Parenting Pauses

Parenting Pauses
Life as a Deaf Parent

by

Dawn Colclasure

Gypsy Shadow Publishing

Parenting Pauses: Life as a Deaf Parent
by
Dawn Colclasure

Gypsy Shadow Publishing, LLC.
Lockhart, TX
www.gypsyshadow.com

Library of Congress Control Number: 2014935418

eBook ISBN: 978-1-61950-193-5
Print ISBN: 978-1-61950-194-2

Published in the United States of America

First eBook Edition: March 7, 2014
First Print Edition: March 12, 2014

Dedication

Dedicated to my children, Jennifer and Jesse, with love. Thanks for making this journey with me.

"For the average hearing person, meeting a deaf person is a novelty, which confronts them with a contrast that fills them with pity. But for deaf people who know nothing else, these expressions of sympathy are jarring and misplaced. They are justifiably frustrated at constantly being made to feel like victims and yearn to be seen as more than just deaf. This may go some way to explaining why there are those who deny that deafness is a disability, but this would be to miss the target of a legitimate complaint. The legitimate complaint is the same as that of anyone who stands out from the crowd for reasons that are beyond their control. People get described as the 'tall guy', the 'fat girl', the 'one with the big nose' and so on, descriptions that obviously overlook virtually everything that's important about a person. Likewise, that 'deaf girl' is never just that. She might also be someone's sister, love animals, have a keen interest in photography, or whatever. She is a complete person."—Mano Zezez

TABLE OF CONTENTS

Introduction

Parenting and deaf parenting. Two similar, yet very different, concepts. Factors of one exist in the other, yet at all times there is one aspect that can only exist on one side: Deafness.

Many times I have been asked what it is like to be a deaf parent. What is it like? It's like wearing earplugs 24/7! But on the other hand, it's that and so much more. A parent who can hear won't experience the same fears, challenges and discrimination a deaf parent will inevitably face. At the same time, a deaf parent will never know some of the joys or experiences their hearing counterpart will enjoy.

The two exist separately, yet together they stand to benefit all the more.

The hearing parent offers advice on a parenting problem the deaf parent is coping with, while the deaf parent offers survival strategies to the hearing parent in picking up on language and social cues observed in the way their child walks and speaks.

But is there really a subcategory of parenting for deaf parents? Is deaf parenting really a subject all its own?

Absolutely.

The world at large may attempt to guide parents along the way, yet when it comes to being able to communicate or facing discrimination, this is where parenting falls short. This is where deaf parenting steps in.

When I became a deaf parent, I knew many challenges lay ahead. I knew there would be sleep deprivation and sick day scares, the same as for any new parent. I knew that communication hurdles lay ahead, that fears for my child's safety would haunt me and that the hearing world would constantly keep watch over how good of a parent I could be. These are the fears of every deaf parent-to-be.

But what I didn't know was just how little there was to help me along the way. There were no clubs to join, no magazines to read, no books to learn from and no videotapes to watch which offered guidance specifically geared toward the deaf parent. I became frustrated over just how little I was able to learn about deaf parenting from the external world. Magazine articles for parents didn't offer alternative solutions to a parent who can't hear, and parenting support groups didn't have somebody accept me as a deaf parent without the constant stares or personal questions.

In essence, I had to learn everything on my own. It wasn't until later that I discovered how I could network with other deaf parents. Writing articles on deaf parenting for *SIGNews*, a national newspaper for the deaf and hard-of-hearing, was just the beginning on my journey toward making deaf parenting less of an issue. Soon I discovered how to face the challenges, cope with my fears and make deaf parenting work. At some point, I was able to fill the void which existed in the book world by providing personal, helpful material in the form of a blog documenting my experiences. I received positive responses to my blog (which, unfortunately at that time, did not provide a way for readers to comment), so I felt, why not expand on this? Turn it all into a book? People wanted to know what it's like to be a deaf parent so I felt I could write a book about it, sharing my own experiences.

This is why I have written this book. If it will help one other deaf parent out there find inspiration, ideas and support, then I am happy to be giving them the one thing I couldn't receive from any other book on the market. There are so many books by *children* of deaf parents who write about their experiences growing up in a deaf home; this is a book from the perspective of a deaf parent with hearing children in the home. Books have been devoted to deaf children, now a book can be devoted to deaf parents.

I am grateful for the opportunity to write about deaf parenting, but the biggest blessing I will always cherish are my experiences as a deaf parent. Of course I would love to be able to hear, but I can't. I am deaf; I accept this. I am a deaf parent; I accept this, too.

Through my experiences as a deaf parent, I have grown stronger, wiser and more informed.

The essays in this book do not cover every issue affecting deaf parenting today. They do cover some major issues, but this is not meant to be a primer on the status of deaf parenting. I offer personal day-in-the-life glimpses of what it's like to be a deaf parent and how I overcome certain challenges, but I am no expert on this particular subject, so what I have said in here should not serve as the final word. Perhaps it can be the subject of research or debate, but nothing in this book must be the absolute truth on any topic covered. Finally, what I write about in this book does not, in any way, represent the opinions and feelings of deaf society as a whole. They are the opinions and feelings of *one deaf person.*

Writing this book has given me a huge sense of fulfillment. I have been inspired and strengthened by the process. I have been given insights on topics I never really thought about before. I hope you will walk away from this book feeling the same way.

—Dawn Colclasure
Eugene, Oregon
February, 2013

Acknowledgments

In this book, I express my gratitude to my mother for her constant support. Other people have provided their support for my journey as a deaf parent as well as for this book:

I would not even be a parent if it weren't for my children, Jennifer and Jesse. Thank you, children, for all of the things you've had to teach me about being your mommy.

Thanks also goes to my husband who, despite his insistence on remaining anonymous and continuing reminders of the importance of privacy, still took the time to offer his opinions and advice on these essays and cheer me on to seeing this manuscript get published.

Thanks to Lisa Abbate, Mridu Khullar and Nancy Marsh for editorial input.

Thanks also to Paula Berman and Emily Hottel King, for additional edits and critiques.

Thanks to Shanta Everington, Deputy Editor of the *Disabled, Pregnancy & Parenting international Journal,* for her never-ending support and encouragement for this book.

Thank you, Raymond Luczak, for making it possible for me to write for *SIGNews*.

Thank you to Katie Prins, David Rosenbaum and Jennifer Dans-Willey, of *SIGNews,* for working with me and for opening the door to my exploration of the world of deaf parenting just from writing about it.

Thanks to John Lee Clark and Kate Tenbeth for comments on the manuscript.

Finally, I would like to say thank you to all of my friends, all of my readers, and all of you deaf parents out there who I have had the pleasure of knowing and networking with. Your constant support has been invaluable to me.

PART ONE:

It's All About Attitude

Hearing or Deaf, the Rules Stay the Same

Something was wrong. My 25-year-old sister stood in the aisle of the grocery store, clutched the pushcart as shock gripped her.

There in the aisle where she stood was a pushcart with a sleeping baby in a seat. No adult who appeared to be the child's parent, or even a family member, was nearby.

"Whose baby is this?" she called out, looking around.

All shoppers in that aisle paid her no mind, going about their business. My sister stayed near the cart, looking around and finding no one who seemed to be responsible for the infant. Finally, a woman entered the aisle, carrying something she'd apparently gone to another aisle to find.

"Is this your baby?" my sister asked.

The woman didn't respond, but only busied herself with arranging the items in her cart to make room for the other item.

Having lived with a deaf person, my sister realized the woman must be deaf. She waved her arm in front of her to get her attention.

"Is this your baby?" my sister repeated, when the woman looked at her, slowly mouthing her words.

The woman answered yes and apologized for not noticing her, saying she was deaf.

"Then why did you leave your baby alone?" my sister demanded.

The woman had no answer. My sister, a parent herself, knew this wasn't right. Whether the woman could hear or not, the baby should not have been left all alone. The fact that the woman was deaf only made the situation worse, yet one has to wonder if this particular woman used her deafness as an excuse to be neglectful. In my twenty-plus years being deaf, I have, unfortunately, known of many deaf and hard-of-hearing people using their deafness as a cop-out to their responsibilities, when what they really lacked was a little common sense.

Once upon a time, I did that very thing.

Since I was 11 years old, my parents have made sure I took responsibility for watching my younger siblings, while also doing my chores. This responsibility didn't change after I lost my hearing. At age 13, I acquired spinal meningitis and lost most of my hearing. Though I had a hearing aid, it helped minimally, and I struggled to accept my deafness. With this new challenge in my life, I suddenly felt helpless. All at once I was dealing with the bullies and peer pressure of junior high school while also trying to communicate and get used to no longer hearing familiar sounds, such as the telephone. I felt sorry for myself, thinking, Oh, no. I'm deaf. I can't do anything anymore. After one episode in which I did a poor job of babysitting my youngest sister, my father let me know otherwise!

One day, my parents left me in charge of my youngest sister, who was almost four years old at the time. My younger brother, who was about nine years old, was also at home, and he kept tabs on just how poor of a job I was doing caring for her. My sister got into one thing after another, all because I'd failed to watch her as closely as I should have. While I busied myself with folding laundry or vacuuming in another room, she was out of my sight. My brother let my father know of my poor babysitting job, even after I cleaned up the messes my sister made, and my father wasn't very pleased. He grabbed a pen, found a piece of paper, instructed me to sit down at the kitchen table and sat in a chair next to mine. He started writing things down, using his typical, large letters in all capitals, reminding me that being deaf didn't give me the excuse to be neglectful. I had duties to perform. Losing my hearing changed nothing. He let me know that I had better find a way to still do the things I had to do in life, including caring for a small child!

When I recall that experience and compare it to what my sister saw at that grocery store that one evening, the message my father tried to convey to me in his bold handwriting hits home. Being deaf is no excuse for being neglectful. Sure, being deaf means that I do things a little differently. And it means I have to watch my children like a hawk, because I must see they are safe, rather than hear it. But everything I do as a deaf parent only reinforces that reminder my father gave to me so long ago.

My deafness is not an excuse for crying victim. We live in a world populated by 64 million deaf and hard-of-hearing people, yet we still see stories on TV, in magazines, on the Internet and in the newspaper of how tragic it is when someone is deaf. The real tragedy is when deafness is allowed to be a barrier in life, which many perceive it to be.

Being deaf changes many things, but it doesn't change the rules of good parenting. It doesn't change the love I have for my children or my determination to meet the responsibilities I have to my family. Babysitting and parenting are like apples and oranges, but that experience taught me an important lesson in what I would someday face as a deaf parent. In my experiences as a deaf parent, I have found a way to take my father's advice just a little bit farther. But my journey in life would not have taken that turn if I hadn't gotten sick with meningitis in the first place.

"Mom? Dawn's Sick"

That fateful Halloween, ten of us went from house to house, and people kept remarking over how many of us there were. We chattered excitedly while standing on the porch of one house, and a man who didn't look very well opened the door. Still smiling, we greeted him with that famous Halloween line, "Trick or Treat!" and held out our bags. The man winced and moved very slowly as he reached into a bowl of treats and placed items into our bags one at a time. I was standing right next to where he was. We left soon after, but I had a lingering bad feeling about him.

The next evening, my sister Elizabeth and I were staying with my older sister Jeanette. I darted about in the courtyard, riding a skateboard and pretending I was Han Solo, while Elizabeth was a storm trooper. "You'll never catch me!" I cried out in my best masculine voice as I rode the skateboard, all the while trying to ignore the pain that pressed down into my neck.

But what I had assumed to be minor neck pain turned into a gripping, numbing pain that went into my lower back. I could hardly walk, and my head started spinning. My sister helped me to her bed and I curled up under the blankets, my teeth chattering. The chills took hold of me, I had a high fever and I kept losing awareness.

When I finally got back home, I couldn't get out of my bed. I kept my eyes closed, because it was hard to see anything. My vision became blurry, and I started having excruciating muscle spasms. Every time the spasms hit, my head twitched and a new wave of pain shot through me. My legs became useless. I was too dizzy to stand up, let alone walk. At one point, when I tried to get out of my parents' bed, I lost my balance and fell backwards, my head hitting the wall as I slumped to the floor.

"Help!" I cried out. But I couldn't hear my voice. I took a deep breath and tried again. "Help!" I just let that sound come out until I heard my voice, but it still only came in as a short sound.

Another day soon after that, as I lay in the bathtub, I tried to raise myself to get out. It was useless. Muscle spasms took over and I couldn't move. Once again, I called for help. Once again, I couldn't hear my voice.

What's wrong with me? I thought. Why can't I hear my voice?

Finally, my parents took me to the hospital. After a painful spinal tap of 15 shots in my spine, for which several nurses had to hold me down, I started to get better.

But I couldn't hear anything. Not a sound. The nurses and doctors talked to me, but I didn't hear a word they said. Their lips would move, but no sound came out. They started to write things down.

At Thanksgiving, I still couldn't hear anything and this tugged at me. I had my very first silent family dinner. Mealtime chatter was lost to me. I couldn't hear the football game on the TV. If music was playing, I had no way of knowing, unless someone told me. It was heartbreaking and I felt that life was so unfair.

After the Thanksgiving festivities, my parents wrote down something on a piece of paper and handed it to me. They explained that I had been sick with meningitis, which is what had caused me to lose my hearing. If they had waited any longer to take me to the hospital, I would have died.

They told me that it was contagious and that the same mustached man who'd given us our Halloween treats had given me this, too.

For several years, I struggled with being deaf. I'd gone from living and enjoying the hearing world to being trapped in a world of silence. Cassette tapes, TV shows and telephone calls all were replaced with feeling music on speakers, reading captions on the TV screen and using a Text Telephone (TTY) to call my friends. I had to change schools and deal with discrimination over being unable to hear people. One of the teachers at the new school made fun of me for being unable to understand her, mockingly repeating the, *huh?* I'd asked when I could not understand her. Another teacher at that same school often complained that my hearing aid was ringing, when I didn't even know it was doing so.

I'd thought a hearing aid would help me to hear again. What a disappointment that it only enhanced sound. I couldn't wear it in the shower or sleep with it on. Not wearing it meant being *completely* deafened again, but I eventually got used to it. It didn't allow for me to hear everything, and it took a while for me to be able to tell where noises came from, but I soon grew to appreciate it. It gave me some small taste of my old life.

When the next Halloween rolled around, I refused to go trick-or-treating. But another Halloween passed, then another, and my family started to get concerned that maybe I was in denial.

They were right. I was trying to stay in a comfort zone, avoiding the fact that *I am deaf.* This was my new reality and I couldn't hide away from it. I wanted to dance to music, I wanted to sing along with my sisters, I wanted to talk to my grandmother on the phone without having to type everything I said. But I couldn't do those things anymore, and I was blaming a stupid holiday ritual for it.

Finally, after five years of boycotting Halloween, I found the strength to venture outside to trick-or-treat again. Elizabeth and I made a big fuss over our costumes and got excited about getting free candy.

A new message had surfaced that night: Life must go on after deafness, no matter what.

Beyond Deaf and Dumb: Coping as a Multi-Disabled Parent

A wave of dread overtook me and fear clutched my heart. They wanted me to *hold* my baby? I couldn't conveniently avoid holding her anymore? I had to actually pick her up by myself and hold her . . . by myself?

No. I couldn't do it. I couldn't take the risk of holding my newborn child in my arms.

What if I dropped her?

Staring at my burned hand that only has three *toe* fingers, noting how my left arm did not hang straight against my side, these thoughts raced through my mind as the nurse busied herself with making my bed. Up until then, they'd changed the baby's diapers. Up until then, they'd held her against me as I tried to nurse her. But now I couldn't avoid the situation anymore.

Now, I had to be the one to hold her. After all, I *was* her mother. A mother is supposed to hold her own baby.

While most parents can't wait to hold their babies after they are born, I could only look at my tiny daughter and be filled with fear. What if I couldn't even hold her? She was so small and she appeared so fragile. Picking her up with my one good hand and my bad hand, I might break her. I might not even be able to hold her.

As I stood there debating the situation, the nurse picked up on my tension. She noticed how

I didn't rush to pick up the baby and hold her in my arms. I don't know if she understood why, but something told her that things were a little uncertain.

It took more than one nurse, my doctor and my husband a good deal of coaxing to get me comfortable enough to try holding the baby. They stayed right next to me as I carefully took her into my arms, gently resting her against my chest. After a few minutes of no baby falling out of my arms, no injury resulting and everything going so perfectly, my terror disappeared and I smiled with joy. I *could* hold my baby! I could do it! She was happy in my arms. She slept so peacefully and she looked so content.

After this, I started to hold her every chance I got. With time and practice, I figured out the best way for me to pick her up and the best way to hold her using my burned left arm. I also figured out how to use my bad hand when I changed her diapers, only after changing *many* diapers.

This experience made me realize I'd been silly to think I couldn't possibly hold my baby because I have a bad hand. That fear of trying to do something so natural for every parent had just been all in my head. That's all it was, just a fear.

My mother often made me recall that story during the times I've run to her because of fear. I was too afraid to pick my baby up, too afraid to leave her sleeping in her crib, too afraid to even take my eyes off of her for just a minute.

But it was only fear holding me back, not the possibility my fears would come true.

I had to remember this the next time something came up that challenged my ability to use both hands well: Give the baby a bath. I worried she'd slip right out of my not-so-perfect grasp. Finally, I decided to just do it.

Before that could happen, however, I had to make sure certain things were in place: The baby's tub was right in front of me so I could get a better grip on her; everything I needed for the bath was nearby; her towel was close, so that I would not be holding a slippery infant for too long after removing her from her tub; and her diaper and clothing items were all within reach of where I dried her off. It took practice, but I figured out the best way to hold her, bathe her and lift her out of the tub. Sometimes it meant getting my T-shirt wet, but it was the best way for me to hold her securely without any accidents.

Quick thinking and focused attention helped me to bathe her without incident.

My next challenge was to figure out the best way to pick her up from a standing position. As she grew, there were many times she wanted me to pick her up and hold her. I had to bend over in a certain way, so I could get my left arm around her securely enough and lift her with my good hand. I probably looked a little silly when I bent over to pick her up, twisting my body a certain way so that I could wrap my left arm around her, but, here again, it's what worked best for us.

It also took practice to figure out the best way to hold her in my arms but, eventually, we worked it out just fine.

The first thing anyone will notice when they see me is not that I am deaf, but that I am physically disabled. Nobody can see my deafness, but they *can* see my physical disability (both are called *physical* disabilities, nonetheless). When they learn that I am also deaf, this changes how they see me. Despite perceptions both good and bad, I've managed to survive so far.

I have never looked at my hand disability as being a *disability*. Actually, it is more of an *injury,* resulting from a car accident I was in at the age of 20 months, in which my left arm, hand, face and back were severely burned. Because of the accident, I have three fingers on my left hand (although they're actually toes). The extensive physical therapy sessions I participated in following several reconstructive surgeries gave me the coping strategies to live life as a normal person. I can still type on the computer, just not as fast as most people. I can still cook a great lasagna and bake a famous cheesecake, which *everyone* in my family constantly requests for special occasions. I can tie my shoes just fine.

But these accomplishments did not prepare me for the biggest challenge ever: Being able to hold a newborn baby. More than this, being able to handle that baby, who would grow bigger and bigger, using both my good hand and my bad hand. There wasn't a physical therapy class offered to instruct me on how to do this, and no book available for me to get ideas. I was on my own to figure that out, yet fear became the only thing standing in my way.

If anyone was able to understand this fear, it was my mother. She had one disability, a result of that very same car accident, in which she lost her left lower leg. She knew all about coping with a disability while trying to parent a child, because she had to do it four more times after that accident. I was only a baby when it happened and even though I was in a coma afterwards, she still had to put up with an active, fussy toddler despite her disability. Almost all of her time parenting her other babies was spent in a wheelchair. I can still see her pushing herself around the house, with two babies on her lap.

After we were in the accident, my mother was being treated for her injuries while I was in a coma. When she was wheeled to where I lay in the room, with wires all over my tiny body, she flew into a rage. She stood on her one remaining leg, lifted her wheelchair over her head, and started screaming as she pounded it against the wall. It took several hospital personnel to calm her down, but that was only the beginning of what my mother knew would be a challenge she had never known before. Our lives had changed forever; we were changed forever. She was now a disabled parent, although the life my mother lived made her perfectly ABLE to go on with her life just fine. Perhaps she was afraid, on some level, but she rarely let me see her cower in fear in the face of a challenge. In fact, I never saw her do that, yet years later she would tell me that she was indeed afraid. It was just a matter of overcoming those fears.

One thing my mom did in order to keep things running smoothly was give the older children responsibilities at an early age. I can only shake my head over 12-year-olds today complaining of boredom while their mothers do all the housework because, when I was that age, I was busy helping out with chores and helping to care for the younger siblings. We didn't like some of the jobs given to us, but my parents made sure we did them, or received punishment. This was a strict rule we all had to follow, and it was just how my mother made sure we, as a family, managed.

I can still remember other things she did which were *survival strategies* as a disabled parent, such as doing something a little slower since she wasn't so adept or physically unlimited, asking for help to move things, and employing the assistance of someone more able-bodied than she was. I remember these things well, using them often as reminders that I, too, must find a way to get things done despite my limitations.

I'm proud of my mother's courage to keep things going despite the physical obstacles she faced. Her strength and determination inspired me. My mother was the one person I went to any time I got frustrated. We'd share stories of how we weren't able to do something and how much this bothered us, the many times we used to cry over being this way, or how we'd turn to God when the frustrations were just too much to bear. My mom would often remind me of how she'd pray if it just got too hard for her to cope, and of how she relied on her faith to see these frustrations through.

She would also remind me that, despite it all, I can't let these disabilities stand in my way. I can't let them prevent me from feeding my child, dressing her, bathing her or even holding her. As a parent, those are my jobs, and disability or no, I have to do them. If she could do them, a person with only one good leg, then I could do them, too, a person with only one good hand.

I had to do them even if fear gripped me and held me back. When I finally conquered that fear of holding my baby for the first time, it was more than just a small victory of being able to hold a tiny baby without trouble. It opened a door in my world as a multi-disabled parent, a door that helped me see that fear was only fear. Fear wasn't what stood in the way. My only obstacle was conquering that fear and doing the things I still had to do.

Paving the Way for Positive Deaf Parenting

"Waaaahhhhh!"

The sound seemed so distant. At first, I wasn't even sure if it was real. Had I heard a baby crying?

I awoke from my slumber and, in a sleepy haze, saw my brother-in-law, Mike, come into my nephew's bedroom, a bottle in one hand and a burp cloth over his shoulder. My sleepy vision wavered as I saw him bend over his son's crib and pick him up, and as I fell back to sleep, thoughts lingered in my mind: *This is what it must be like to be awakened by a baby's cry at night. That's probably what I'll go through someday when I'm a parent, too.*

Several months later, I caught meningitis and lost my hearing. After I recovered from that experience, I knew one thing: Now I'll never be awakened by a baby's cry at night.

Or, so I thought.

Then I gave birth. Then I had to go home with the baby, no longer able to sleep at night with the security of the hearing nurses being alerted to the baby's cries to awaken me.

Now, I was on my own. My husband and I both were. A hearing person did not live with us. It was just us two deaf parents with a hearing, crying baby.

How would we ever sleep, knowing we might not awaken to our baby's cries when she needed us?

At first, I didn't sleep. I wore my hearing aid 24/7. Even though the hearing aid doesn't help me to hear things the same way a hearing person hears things, it *does* help me distinguish the sound I heard coming from my daughter's mouth from a noise on the TV. I was amazed I could *hear* her cry; it really *did* have a *waah* sound! Yet even more amazing was a step back in time to when my nephew's infant cries had awakened me that night, because now my own infant's cries were waking me. Thanks to wearing the hearing aid as I slept, and keeping the baby in a bassinet right next to my bed, I woke up when she cried at night. Problem solved!

Still, I knew it wasn't a good idea to sleep with my hearing aid on. I wasn't too clear on why this was bad, just that it wasn't a good idea. Added to this was my knowledge that this *miracle* wasn't going to last forever. Even though we were shelling out money for new hearing aid batteries as the hearing aid did continue to help me wake up when I heard the baby's cries, it was too risky to rely on it long-term. What if I slept the whole night through with my hearing aid on, and I didn't wake up when the baby cried? I just didn't want to push my luck.

The first thing I did was talk this over with my family. "What can I do to help me wake up at night when the baby cries? I can't rely on the hearing aid all the time." I talked with my mother, my sisters, my mother-in-law. This kind of thing was so new for all of us, given that my husband and I were the only deaf people in our families. None of them knew of any way to handle this.

I hit the Internet and started searching. Some deaf parents posted about how they'd sleep with their arm on their babies, but this was not something I could safely rely on either. After all, we do move around in our sleep! That's exactly what happened when I tried that one night, still wearing the hearing aid. Forget that idea!

I needed something more reliable, more tangible. I needed . . . something techie. After all, I used a TTY to make phone calls. Surely, there existed another tech device for a deaf parent with an infant needing to be fed at 3:00 in the morning.

I eventually found out about a place called the Center on Deafness, located in Riverside, California. I called them and talked with a representative about my situation. I said I was looking for some kind of *baby monitor* just for a sleeping deaf parent.

"You mean the Baby Cryer?" he asked.

"What is a Baby Cryer?" I asked.

He explained it's a device with a sound sensor that works with a vibrational rod, which you put under the mattress. The more he explained it to me, the more I thought, *No way does that work!* It sounded complicated, but I was willing to check it out all the same. He gave me a link to go to on the Web, where I could learn more about it.

After the phone call, I visited the website and started reading all about this *Baby Cryer* thing. I started visiting other sites to read what other deaf parents had to say about the Baby Cryer and was encouraged by their glowing remarks.

Well, I'll give it a shot, I decided. It's better than nothing.

The next thing I did was contact a company selling the Baby Cryer. "I am a new deaf parent," I typed on my TTY. "I heard about the Baby Cryer and was wondering if I could order one from your company."

They made things easier. They suggested I get information about a local hearing device retailer and they'd ship the Baby Cryer there, where I could pay for it.

My mother-in-law ended up paying for it. Once she heard about this situation, she immediately got involved and generously helped us arrange for the Baby Cryer to be shipped to a local hearing aid store. Once she got one to us, we all rejoiced, yet I was still skeptical. Was this thing even going to work?

My husband, being the tech whiz, set up the Baby Cryer in our bedroom. Next, he explained what this device was all about. The Baby Cryer actually connected to our Sonic Boom alarm clock, which has a vibrating rod kept under the mattress which vibrates when the alarm goes off. The Baby Cryer's sound sensor was placed next to the baby's bassinet, and being connected to the alarm clock, the vibrational rod would act as both our alarm to wake us up at a certain time and for when the baby cried.

The first night we tried it, it was a miracle I even recognized the shaking bed as anything other than a product of an earthquake. Having spent most of my life in California, I was used to earthquakes, but a mini-earthquake happened every time the baby woke up crying and the vibrational rod went off under the mattress. Wow! It *really* worked! What an amazing device for the deaf!

Figuring out a solution to this problem was just the first step I took in finding solutions to other problems as a deaf parent. My confidence in being able to manage this deaf parenting stuff grew. We can do it! We have the technology!

That confidence in overcoming obstacles was just one factor of deaf parenting I knew I wanted to keep. I wanted it to be a permanent part of our adventures as deaf parents.

Still, I had a lot more things to learn. Figuring out how to sleep at night without the hearing aid on and still being awakened to a crying baby was just the beginning, especially after the skin in my inner ear became inflamed and I couldn't wear a hearing aid anymore.

We were in *complete* deafness now. There was no sound, at all. And no hearing aid to help us out.

Instead of getting scared, I just dealt with it. I kept that confidence in the picture. There are so many other deaf parents out there who survive without the assistance of a hearing aid, caring for their hearing children without being able to hear them at all, and if they have managed, I can manage, I told myself.

But I needed to know just *how* to manage first.

That's where the networking came in. I joined an online group of deaf parents and we talked parenting. Eventually, I landed a job writing about deaf parenting for *SIGNews*, a newspaper for the deaf and hard-of-hearing. This opened the door to more educational experiences and more networking.

By writing about deaf parenting for *SIGNews*, my confidence in my abilities grew stronger, because now I had a way to address the same concerns other deaf parents had. Writing about home signs, which are not actually ASL (American Sign Language) signs, but signs personally created and used among family members, helped me figure out how to use home signs without threatening the importance of using ASL in the home with my own child. Ditto when I wrote about common fears deaf parents faced and what kind of tech gadgets were the favorites among deaf parents. It just really opened doors for helping me to navigate this journey.

Writing about deaf parents speaking out for their rights and keeping a positive relationship with their children hammered home more messages: I had to speak out for my rights as a parent, too. If discrimination was taking place or rights were being violated, I had to stand up and say something about it, just as other deaf parents were saying something about it. I had to keep my relationship with my child positive and worry-free.

And, finally, the overall impact of what I was doing made deaf parenting such a bigger deal now. I was writing about things going on with deaf parenting, and doing things to overcome obstacles. This had to be something my child would someday appreciate. As a parent, I knew I was a role model to her. I had to model a can-do attitude in the face of deafness, while also doing something productive.

But was I meeting that goal? Even as I wrote those articles and did the best I could in finding solutions, I had to wonder: Would it pay off?

There was no way for me to tell for sure. And, at the age of two, Jennifer could not really express to me her approval, or even her disapproval, of what I was doing to create a lasting, positive and inspirational relationship with her as her deaf mother.

Even still, I planted the seeds. It was just a matter of time to watch those seeds take root and see if, indeed, I was on the right path.

PART TWO:

The Realities of Deaf Parenting

Helping Hands, Helping Ears

A hand pats my back as I rinse off a plate in the sink. I turn to look at my sister. "Jennifer said she wants spaghetti and juice for dinner," she informs me.

"Did she just tell you that?" I ask, noticing Jennifer is not in the kitchen.

My sister smiles as she nods. "As she walked out of the kitchen, she said 'I want spaghetti and juice for dinner.'"

As I mentally note the dinner request, I sigh silently. Apparently, Jennifer getting my visual attention when she speaks is not as consistent as I'd hoped. With a hearing person in the house, she thinks it's perfectly fine to speak to them orally and have them convey the message.

Did she get Jennifer's attention visually before speaking? *I had to be sure.*

"Did she look at you when she said that?" I ask my sister, holding my breath.

My sister shakes her head. "I was standing over there when she walked out."

Ah, there it was.

On one hand, in situations like these, I was grateful Jennifer adapted so easily. On the other, however, I wondered if this kind of switch was a good idea. After all, I wanted her to get used to the way we, her deaf parents, needed her to communicate with us, which included using home signs and speaking directly to us, face to face. *Were we confusing her?*

The question lingered after several rounds of her being cared for by her deaf parents alternating with being monitored by her hearing grandparents and relatives. At home, there was face-to-face communication and home signs. But at Grandma's house, she could tell her grandmother things from another room and watch her actually speaking and listening on the telephone. But after she began to forget certain signs, I started to worry.

First-time parents should not be afraid of asking for help. In fact, I'd be surprised to meet any first-time parent who'd *never* asked for help! There's no way to know everything before it comes up. Mothers, mothers-in-law and sisters who are parents all know this and they're ready and willing to help out when there's a new baby in the house. (It would be nice if they'd help without passing judgment on how clueless or incapable we are, but we can't have everything!)

My mom was a *huge* help for me. When Jennifer was an infant, the combination of deaf and hearing caregivers was not so much an issue. My mom bathed my daughter, fed her, burped her, dressed her and put her down for a nap, and to Jennifer, it might as well have been me doing this. Her perceptions of living with deaf parents and using the communication strategies needed were issues to tackle farther on down the road.

And when we finally did reach that point, I started mentally to take notes on how things were different.

For almost every occasion, her father watched her when I had to go to a doctor appointment or run some other errand. But there were times one of my sisters or even my mother watched the baby. As Jennifer was learning the ropes of living with deaf parents, differences began to show. After I'd picked her up, she'd start talking without looking at me. She didn't remember to use the signs and often forgot to get our attention when she wanted to tell us something. One time when I was watching the TV, she walked up to me, patted my arm and, when I looked at her, she asked, "Why didn't you answer me?" When I asked her what she meant, she explained she'd been at the table calling to me. It had not been that long since I had last looked at her to *check* on her with my eyes as I watched a TV program, but it had been long enough for her to be calling to me and getting no response.

I started to make it a point to *go over the rules* when we got home. I reminded her that she had to look at me when she spoke, I reviewed the signs we'd taught her so she could use them again, and I made it a point to reacquaint her with the way we did things at home, such as feeling the speakers, using a TTY and having the captions on for TV shows.

Despite the confusion, I was still grateful. Jennifer is a hearing child, after all, and these experiences gave her the chance to interact with the hearing world. She could relax and talk to someone who was in a different room. She learned to talk on a telephone the same way a hearing person would. She exercised the part of her brain active during verbal speech and, best of all, did all of those fun things the hearing community enjoys: Sing along with songs, dance to music and play games with neat sound effects.

Another bonus: the hearing person caring for her—whether it was my sister or my mother—could gauge how well Jennifer's speech was developing. They could correct her if she said a word wrong and help her pronounce a word she didn't know. Even better, they could help her expand her vocabulary. Of course, they laughed over her baby talk and shared a funny way she said a word, but they also acted as monitors to just how well she spoke by encouraging her to talk more than she signed around them.

Some disabled parents may see all of this the wrong way. Allowing a hearing person to be in charge would invite judgment or criticism over the deaf parent's abilities to competently care for the child (and, believe me, we did have our share of it!). It's as though the child is placed in a chair with a bright light shining in their face, with the hearing relatives grilling her for dirty laundry. *Is your mother feeding you? Is she keeping the house clean? Are you able to watch TV with the sound on?*

One of the times I experienced criticism from a hearing relative was when they observed how I cared for Jennifer. There was a time my sister let me know in an email that things didn't look right. Jennifer was six years old.

My sister wrote in her email: Please do look into getting a hearing aid. When you guys were visiting, there were a few times when Jennifer came up to you and said something or asked you a question and you thought she said something else and she kept saying, "No, that's not what I'm saying." and you just brushed her off or assured her about something completely different than what she was saying. Jennifer might get to a point where she doesn't feel the need to talk to you that much because you two have a lack of communication or you just won't understand. What happens if someone molests her at school or something? Who can she talk to?

I had to remind my sister that my daughter and I have communication techniques in place, and that I won't be able to understand her 100% of the time when she only communicates with me verbally. That's the way it is with everybody who does not elect to use sign language when communicating with me. I am not a perfect lipreader and sometimes things get misunderstood. It happens.

She already knows she is able to talk to me about everything, I replied to the email. Communication is just a little bit slower, and we work through things. She is starting to fingerspell more often now, which really helps. We recently had something that happened (not to HER) and it brought on a serious discussion and there were communication bumps, but we found a way to get through that.

I didn't want to get into a big discussion about it, my sister replied. But either way according to

YOU the discussion went well, how do you know Jen just didn't give up and say, "Yes," or, "OK," just to end the conversation because her mom just didn't get it? According to you, you guys get through bumps. You don't really know that for sure though.

This was my response: You and (deleted) only spent a few hours with us. This, I feel, was not a sufficient amount of time for you to judge how I am able to communicate with my daughter. Or not communicate with her, in some cases. Yes, we have times in which we misunderstand each other. We have times in which Jennifer will say, "Oh forget it," or just end the conversation out of frustration. Believe me, I know. I'm not stupid about things like this. I've been deaf long enough to know when people have decided to just end a conversation when the communication isn't so good. Parenting is not a perfect job, (deleted). We all make mistakes. Jennifer and I tend to work out our communication problems —and we DO work them out. If there's a problem, I'm usually able to pick up on it. It's just something that can be detected after being deaf for so long. But there WILL be times when things don't work out and we are not understanding each other as well as we should be.

Despite my irritation over being called to court over that *one* mistake, which is actually something we work out on our own as mother and daughter, I knew my sister was right about one thing. I *didn't* know for sure if Jennifer and I got through our communication bumps. All I knew was that we tried.

We make an effort to communicate. She *does* tell me, "That's not what I said," if I misunderstand her, and sometimes I need to put my foot down and tell her to *please* repeat what she said to me so that I understand her better.

Despite that negative side of what could happen when hearing relatives care for my child, I'm still convinced it is good for Jennifer to have the hearing world be a part of her life, too, just as the deaf world is.

As long as I remembered to refresh her memory on what she needed to do when communicating with us, it seemed to work out okay. She wasn't so confused anymore and, in fact, she seemed more relaxed and content with life. I relaxed in being assured that a hearing person was there to pick up on any dangers I could not see. The best part is that, after a while, I didn't have to remind her how to communicate with us anymore. She understands these two worlds she's a part of. She eventually figured it all out on her own and became flexible enough to handle both environments just fine. Life found a way.

"Mommy Can't Hear."

The volume on the TV was too loud. I knew this because I felt the sound vibrations. I moved to turn the TV down, placing my hand on the speaker to feel how loud the volume was. Since the TV set didn't have a numerical indicator on the volume level, this was my only way to determine whether the volume was too high.

It wasn't long before I noticed Jennifer doing the same thing. Before she turned two, I noticed she, too, placed her hand on the TV's speaker and then turned down the sound. As I watched this, my heart leapt. Was this an indicator that, finally, she understood why I did this? Did she finally know that I can't hear, so use this method to judge the volume on the TV?

But, no. I realized, with that familiar sinking feeling, that she was only imitating me. She was imitating my movements, not doing something which a deaf person does because of the inability to hear. She was just doing what all toddlers do: Imitating.

I'd hoped my daughter was finally grasping something that was a part of my deaf world. I'd tried many times in the past to explain to her, "Mommy can't hear." I might as well have been saying something like, "It's a nice day today," or speaking to her in a foreign language, because no matter how often I'd try to get this through to her, her young mind just didn't *get* it. Many times, following my verbal exchange with her, she'd still look at me confused over why I didn't jump up to answer the door right away, or why I didn't realize she was crying until I actually *saw* her crying.

This little drawback left me feeling frustrated. I wanted her to understand that the reason why was because I'm deaf. She didn't know I was without something she didn't realize could be taken away. Trying to explain to an eighteen month old all about deafness was like trying to explain the mechanics involved in building a space shuttle to her. Every single word just went right over her head.

So I tried using other ways to get her acquainted with how life is different. I'd show her how I used a TTY to make phone calls, left the captioning on the TV turned on and said, "I can't understand it," when something without captioning came on. I let her see me looking out the window to see if someone was at the door. For the last one, I'd say "Is there someone knocking?" as I looked out the window or I'd feel the door and ask the question if I *thought* someone had knocked.

After she turned two, I think it finally started to register with her that *Mommy can't hear.* It also was a possibility to her that Daddy couldn't hear, either, because she noticed the same things about him: He used sign language to communicate, he didn't respond to a door knock right away and he, too, placed his hand on the speaker of the TV before adjusting the volume. Pretty soon she started to realize there was a specific reason why we did these things, and that they were things which she really didn't need to do herself. Still, even as she saw us doing these things, and even imitating them (as a baby, she'd imitate, in her own way, the signs we made to each other), she didn't really understand it was because we are deaf.

As she got older, I'd try and try again to explain to her that Mommy couldn't hear her. I spent a long time trying to decide the best way to talk to her about it. I'm no child psychologist or parenting coach, so I was confused: What was the best approach to take in handling something like this? She was still so young and vulnerable. Simply saying something like, "Mommy can't hear," wasn't enough to get her to understand that I can't hear anything. Simply watching me, she caught onto the fact that I responded to sound differently and that I used things other people didn't use when making a phone call or watching TV.

I still felt I needed to talk to her about it, though. I needed to cover all of the bases with her, and answer any questions she might have. I mentally went over a conversation many times, trying to figure out just exactly what to cover. I finally decided that the conversation would focus on how I became deaf, what kind of tools I used in daily life (a TTY, closed-captioning device, text pager), and what being deaf means to our world and how we live. Being deaf means not being able to go to an uncaptioned movie and it means having to use the TTY to make a phone call. I kept in mind that I shouldn't allow this topic to impose a negative mood or unneeded drama. I did not want to imply that being deaf is *bad.* I'd be in a calm, optimistic mood and speak to her in a normal tone of voice. I'd also be sure to keep in mind that knowing I can't hear might make her feel afraid, as though I wouldn't be able to take care of her so well. I'd have to be sure to address this concern and assure her there are little ways we still manage to ensure her safety.

I also realized it would be best if I had this conversation with her without the assistance of someone to *interpret* for me. Of course, I would want her to realize that sometimes Mommy needed the help of an ASL interpreter at doctor appointments or things like that, but not right now. There *had* been times one of my sisters or parents helped me out in understanding what she said, but because we were going to have a talk about something so crucial, I felt it was best if we had it one-on-one. Having someone to help me understand what she said might cause some confusion or send her the wrong signal. It might tell her that I needed someone who *could* hear to ensure we communicated okay.

So one day, when she was three years old, I sat down with her and told her the following:

"You've probably noticed how I don't hear things so good. Do you understand why I don't answer the door when someone knocks or tell the dog to be quiet when he barks? It's because I can't hear those things. I can't hear anything at all, because I am deaf. But you don't need to worry about anything, okay? I am using things to help me know when there are sounds and they will help me to take care of you. They will let me know when someone is at the door or when there is a fire in the house. I can still take good care of you because of these things, so you don't need to be afraid. And I promise I'll do my best to be there for you anytime you need me and that I won't miss anything that you need me to see. And if we use sign language to talk with, we can talk anytime you want to."

During that exchange, I often paused to ask her, "Do you understand?" and, "Okay?"

I needed to know she was on the same level as I tried to tell her, in words she knew, that deafness is a part of our lives and always will be. Deafness would affect how we lived and meant our lives would be just a little bit different than everybody else's.

She seemed to get through this talk okay and I noticed later on how she wasn't the same anymore. From that moment on, she'd pat my back to get my attention, point at the door if somebody knocked and run to get me if something fell off of a shelf.

This helped me to realize something: Children will *eventually* understand that a parent can't hear. For a while, Jennifer just didn't understand this. When she was so young, she took her hearing for granted, never understanding that it was something that could be taken away or that it was something a lot of people lived without. She didn't easily grasp that her parents didn't hear like she did; it took her a while to *get it.* I think my opening the door to this fact of our lives helped her. I answered all of her questions and showed her how life was different for us. I think that's ultimately what helped her to finally realize that Mommy and Daddy are deaf. Most important, she finally realized what being *deaf* means.

One day, after she was four years old, I finally got proof that she understood the concept that being deaf means I can't hear. While giving her a bath and washing her up, I talked about the movie, *The Last Unicorn*, that we were planning to watch together the next day. "You'll like the song that plays in the movie," I said, rinsing the soap from her shoulders. "It has really good music."

"But how do you know?" she asked. "You're deaf."

I smiled, inwardly thanking my lucky stars at how she finally understood what exactly the word *deaf* meant.

"Well, that's because I used to hear that song, Jennifer," I answered. "Mommy hasn't always been deaf."

That right there was a whole new topic for us to discuss. But at least, at this point, she was armed with the knowledge that her parents are deaf, and what being deaf is really all about. *Baby steps,* I told myself. She'd have to understand one thing before moving on to the next.

In any event, I knew I couldn't leave her in the dark about my deafness. I knew I had to take some time to talk with her about it and answer any questions she might have. I'm no child psychologist, but at least I handled this kind of thing in a way I thought was best. It worked for us, obviously, but there was still a whole lot more we'd have to explore later on down the road. At least we were on that road, and at least she understood what kind of road it was.

Suspicious Eyes

A mood of merriment lingered in the room. As my mother sat in a chair across from me, Jennifer happily played with her toys on the floor. Then she gradually brought herself up on her feet and happily tumbled through the room. She'd recently just started walking and my mother and I laughed as we watched her take those wobbly steps. Both my mother and I recognized this as just my one-year-old daughter once again trying to walk without falling, and we were both slightly disappointed when she tumbled to the floor. My father, who'd been standing in the room, saw this unfold and grabbed it as an opportunity once again to give me the same warning he'd been giving me ever since Jennifer was born: "You have to *watch* her."

The happy mood faded away. A bit of irritation and anger started to prick at me as I wanted to scream, "I *was* watching her! She was right in front of me! It's not my fault she fell down!"

Still, I bit my tongue, just as I did every time my father would be all over a scene with warnings of how I have to stay *on top* of things, since I'm a deaf parent. I pushed aside memories of how he'd reminded me that someone would pick up the phone and call Child Protective Services (CPS) if they saw Jennifer with a bump on her head. Instead, I focused my attention on helping my daughter up off the floor.

Once again, I was reminded of how my father was judging just how good of a parent I could be. Because of his constant warnings and remarks, I had to think that maybe he acted this way because I am deaf. After all, he didn't get in any of my other siblings' faces after they became parents. Drug abuse? Violence? Neglect? Oh, that was all stuff he was willing to overlook. But DEAFNESS! My Lord, the child was doomed!

It hadn't helped that he'd acted so aloof and standoffish every time my pregnancy had been discussed. In fact, there were times he'd left the room.

Did he act this way because I was deaf? I couldn't help but wonder. Part of me thought so, since he seemed to constantly stress how my being deaf meant the world at large would suddenly put me and the baby underneath some kind of giant magnifying glass.

That's the message he kept sending me in one way or another, and it ended up being a message I started to carry around with me. Okay, so I had to be careful when the world saw me with my baby. It didn't matter that no one would pick up right away that I am a deaf parent; my obvious physical disability is enough to make people stare.

In a perfect world, nobody would stare. Nobody would point, ask questions or keep watching me to see if (and when) I screw up.

No matter how much I might try to make everything pan out and everything work, this conviction wasn't easy for me to shake off. My father kept hammering it into my head: Being a disabled parent meant I had to be careful. It meant that

I was more susceptible to CPS swooping in and taking away my baby, all because I am deaf!

Granted, there were times I screwed up. But, you know what? Every parent, whether they are deaf or can hear, blind or can see, has the occasional mistake. Heck, even my own parents made mistakes sometimes. All parents do. When I screwed up in front of someone and got reprimanded for it, I could only grit my teeth and think, *They're not exactly perfect, either.*

This was so true for certain other members of my family. Over the years of being a deaf parent, CPS never bothered me. I *did* have an interview with a social worker after my second child was born, but no one, and I mean *no one,* came to me and said, "You know what? This deaf parenting thing you're trying to pull off just isn't working for your children. We're removing them from your care." That ended up happening to three of my siblings, who are *not* deaf and *not* disabled in any way, but it never happened to me.

It wasn't just the warnings to watch out for CPS that I had to deal with during my daughter's early years. My parents checked in with us every so often, offering to have a hearing sibling spend a few days in our home and repeatedly reminding me of how I couldn't mess up.

All the same, I knew I had to take heed of my father's warnings. It's true that being a disabled parent puts me under greater scrutiny. It's true that the hearing community will keep tabs on just how good of a job I am doing as a parent. When a hearing parent screws up, other hearing parents pat their shoulders with words of how it happens to them, too. But if a deaf parent screws up, we get criticized and it opens the door to being judged. One hearing doctor I visited, for example, had a hard time accepting me as a disabled parent. On top of refusing an interpreter for me and refusing to write things down so I could understand what he said, he kept wanting to know how I managed to communicate with my child since I am deaf.

This is my world as a deaf parent. As much as I try to tell myself that this isn't true, the reality is that, as a disabled parent, I have a lot to prove. Even as the hearing community is doing things like this with the understanding that it's for my children's best interests, I know what's really going on here: I'm being told that my deafness is a problem.

I realize it's not like we're living in the kind of world in Orwell's *1984,* but even in my own family and in my own neighborhood, I am still being watched. Big Brother isn't so much the city or the hospitals; it's my parents, my siblings, my neighbors.

I know I'm not the perfect parent. Sometimes, Jennifer gets into things. Sometimes, I don't catch something she says. But that doesn't make me a bad parent. It doesn't doom her to a life of accidents or communication problems.

Deaf parenting takes a lot of work. I went through a lot of trial and error to find the best way to be a good deaf parent. I didn't learn everything I needed to know in the beginning, but you know what? No first-time parent does. You can't judge whether a person can be a good parent based on their ability to hear, see, move or talk. Blind parents have been taking care of their kids for years. So have deaf parents. We have found ways to adapt. Our lives may seem different, our living conditions strange, but we work to be great parents to our kids. We *want* to be great parents to our kids! We make every effort to ensure that we are good parents, an effort that would still be there if we were not disabled.

I have been lucky. So far, CPS hasn't come knocking on my door, and nobody has tried to take my babies away. With this constant watch over me, however, I know I'm not yet out of the woods. In fact, this only reminds me never to let my guard down and think we'll be okay, because something tells me that we won't.

Coping With Fears as a Deaf Parent

Sleep was elusive. I tossed and turned in bed, trying to relax and push aside the horrible images haunting my mind. Some intruder had climbed through my child's bedroom window and was hurting her. Or snatching her away. Or reaching for their knife. Or . . .

That was enough. I jumped out of bed and ran to my daughter's room, holding my breath. I carefully peeked inside of her dark bedroom to find her . . . sleeping peacefully in her crib. No monsters were under her bed. No intruder was lurking in the dark. She was fine.

Despite this reassurance, many nights passed where I dealt with those same worries as we retired for the night. I'd try to assure myself that, with a Baby Cryer, we'd be alerted to any sounds in her room. But someone sneaking into her room would be extra quiet, quiet enough not to set off the Baby Cryer. At least, that's what I thought. And just as I kept waking up at odd hours on the night Jennifer was born, feeling panic or anxiety about whether she was okay, I kept having many nights of restless sleep. It was bad enough that the first six weeks had me walking in a sleep-deprived haze. Now, even after she'd started to sleep through the night in her own room, sleep was impossible.

When I explained this situation to my mother-in-law, she could only laugh and shake her head, years of experience showing in her eyes.

"You'll never get any sleep," she said. "Even when my sons were older, even when they turned 16, I never got any sleep."

Wow, parents can barely sleep even when their kids are older? I remembered puzzling over this for a long time. Surely, they wouldn't worry so much about their child's safety at night when they are 12 years old, 16 years old, or even 18 years old. That didn't sound right.

But in a way, it made sense.

Now I know just how terrifying it is to trust some higher power to watch over all of us as we sleep each night. Even so, we the parents are responsible for ensuring the child's safety. After years as a parent, I finally understood the fear so many parents go through.

On the other hand, my situation was different. That's what I was thinking on the day I had that talk with my mother-in-law. My own fear of sleeping at night while my child slept in another room was even more pronounced because I couldn't hear anything! Baby Cryer or no, what if something happened?

I didn't get into details about that concern with my mother-in-law that day. I wasn't sure if she'd understand this. I just went through several nights of waking up to check on the baby, or even finally resigning myself to trusting the Baby Cryer to alerting us when there was a noise in her room. But I'd make sure that trust could indeed be in place: I turned up the sensitivity level on the sound sensor. In fact, I turned it all the way up. Then one day, my husband sneezed outside of the opened door of our daughter's room, only to notice the lamp flashing on our bedroom table as the Baby Cryer went off. He told me it shouldn't be up so high and that's when I let it all out: I was terribly afraid to sleep at night if it wasn't turned all the way up. What if something happened to the baby while we were sleeping?

This led to a long talk about safety at night. He assured me that as long as we were taking every measure possible to keep our home and baby safe, that was the best we could do. Make sure windows and doors were locked securely, make sure nothing is preventing the Baby Cryer from doing its job without turning it all the way up, make sure the baby's bed was safe for her to sleep in and that we had a light or two on in the house. My own personal must-have for home security? A dog.

Thanks to that talk and double-checking on the security of our home, I started to feel better about going to sleep at night. I just had to put my faith in the fact we'd done everything possible to ensure the baby was safe. This is how other parents cope with that fear, so we'd follow suit. And everything turned out fine in the end.

This was just one common fear we had to deal with. Others followed. What if something happens to Jennifer while I'm in the bathroom? I started to make sure someone was with her when I used the bathroom or I would take her into the bathroom with me.

Years later, however, I learned an important lesson about making sure someone was with her when I had to use the bathroom.

At my sister's house in Lake Arrowhead, I checked to see that Jennifer was playing with her cousins in the living room and that my sisters and parents were nearby. I ducked into the bathroom and when I came out, she was gone. At first I thought she was hiding, because she liked to hide. But soon enough, panic gripped me as I went all over the house and I couldn't find her. I started to run around, screaming out her name, my eyes darting everywhere for her. My family noticed my panic and started looking for her, too. Eventually, one of my older nephews found her—in the woods! Apparently, she and two of her cousins had decided to wander off into the woods in the backyard, without telling anyone. My dad came up to me, caught my attention and gave his typical reminder: "You have to watch her."

It was then that I finally found my voice. I looked at my father and said, "I had to use the bathroom." I wanted to say more things to him at that moment, such as: *Can't I even use the bathroom for two minutes without somebody getting on my back about not seeing where my daughter is?* Or *what was everybody else doing while I was away? Nobody else could keep an eye on her for two minutes?*

But, instead, what I defended myself with seemed to get through to him that I couldn't watch my child like a hawk 24/7.

I understood the lesson of this experience very clearly: If I leave her with someone when I use the bathroom, I have to tell them, "I'm going to use the bathroom real quick. Please keep an eye on Jennifer for me."

Fortunately, later on down the road, some family members finally understood they had to keep an eye on Jennifer while I had to step away to use the bathroom. Some of them even insisted

I not take her in the bathroom with me, that she'd be fine with them while I was gone.

Another fear I had to deal with was the possibility something could happen to my child when I wasn't looking. What if she got into something she shouldn't while I was in another room? I baby-proofed her room like crazy and did the same for the rest of the house after she started climbing up on a glass table, and picking things up off of shelves.

Next, I had to deal with safety hazards in the kitchen. At first, we used a baby gate to keep her from going into a room too dangerous for her to be in. If she was in another room while I was in the kitchen, her dad was usually with her. Or someone else. After she outgrew the baby gate, I put all plastics and other *safe* objects into the lower cabinets in the kitchen. She'd often busy herself playing with bowls or stacking canned goods while I stood nearby doing the dishes or preparing a meal. I kept her away from the stove and always within view if we both had to be in the kitchen at the same time. And always when the stove was on, I'd get her attention, point at the stove and say, "Hot! Don't touch!"

When I wasn't comfortable with this arrangement, I'd set her up in her highchair with a snack, or at the table with a coloring book and crayons, so I could monitor her as I cooked in the kitchen. It helped that she was where I could see her as I worked.

This take-charge approach helped me cope with common fears every deaf parent faces. Of course, some fears could not be resolved. It took time to figure out how to overcome those fears, talking with others and, very often, just having faith that things would be okay.

Still, there were other fears I had no control over. What if she likes the *cooler parents* who can dance with their kids to music or talk with them on the telephone better? Well, I just had to be okay with that and let her enjoy those things, because they *are* a part of her hearing world. What if she grows weary of having to sign to us or look at us when she's talking? We'd figure out another way to communicate, just like we always have. What if she starts saying things she shouldn't be saying when we don't see her, only because she knows she can get away with it? I had to accept that things like that could happen, because there really wasn't anything I could do about it, short of reminding her to watch her language. And, anyway, even kids of hearing parents do that. They'll swear or gossip when their parents aren't within earshot. That's just life.

Even so, other fears existed later on down the road. Just as I've found solutions to the fears I have now, I know I'll find a solution to the very real fears I will have to cope with later. It was just a matter of picking my battles. I know those kinds of worries will crop up someday, but for the time being, I have to take care of the worries that exist in the here and now. Other problems lie ahead as my children grow older, but I'll cross that bridge when I come to it.

Breaking Through Communication Barriers: Pointing, Showing and Asking

For a brief moment, I had a connection with hearing parents. A sigh escaped through my lips, a sense of frustration tugged at me and I shook my head.

Ah, hearing parents must go through this, too, I thought. Just as we all go through the sleep deprivation, temper tantrums from our little ones, messy diapers, sick babies, fears and anxieties over home security, and stubbornness.

And mumbling children. Let us not forget the mumbling children.

You parents know what I mean. Those little children who mumble-mumble every time we ask them a question or try to figure out what it is that is bothering them.

I stared at my mumbling child, whose lips seemed glued together as she spoke, and pondered this connection. Just as a hearing parent would try to discern just *what* the mumbling child is trying to say, I, too, tried to understand what words were coming out of my child's mouth. And, as a deaf parent, I tried not to take this personally.

Still, a thought ran through my mind: I'm her mother, for God's sakes! Why can't I understand her?

This wasn't happening because I was deaf, I reminded myself. She's just mumbling, making it impossible for me to read her lips!

"Jennifer," I said, trying to speak in as calm a voice as I could. "Please tell me again what you're trying to say to Mommy."

Mumble-mumble-mumble.

"What?"

Mumble-mumble-mumble.

I sighed and sat back in my chair. "I'm sorry, Baby. I don't understand what you're trying to say."

Frustration took over her once-shy demeanor. My then two-year-old stomped her foot, pumped her fists through the air and gave me a determined look. "Shoes!" she cried out. "I can't find my sneakers!"

It's easy to get frustrated when trying to understand what a mumbling child is saying. The many times Jennifer and I have had this difficulty, we just had to stop everything and take a deep breath. We try to find an alternative method to communicate. For some reason, she resorted to mumbling an awful lot when she was a toddler, so I had to take it into my own hands to figure out how to communicate effectively.

The next time a mumbling episode happened, I was busy giving her a bath.

As she splashed around in the bathtub, playing with her toys, I started to think about what to give her for lunch. Since I couldn't decide on anything, I figured I'd ask her.

That took a little more effort.

"What do you want for lunch?" I asked her.

Jennifer just continued to play with her toys, undistracted by my question.

"Jen!" I called, clapping my hands to get her attention.

She looked up with a smile.

"What do you want for lunch?" I repeated.

A series of mumbling, lips glued together, talk happened before she went back to playing with her toys.

"Jen!" I called again. More clapping. When I got her attention, I decided to ask something else. "Do you want some chicken noodle?"

Mumble-mumble. More playing.

Again I clapped and called out her name. Do you want a hot dog? Grilled cheese? Macaroni and cheese?

When I finally suggested something she liked, she eagerly nodded her head in response before going back to playing in the tub.

I didn't just solve the lunch mystery that day. Something else struck me. I had an idea.

The next time we had a mumbling episode, I tried something different to understand what she was saying. These ideas developed into great communication strategies complementing her learning experience of sign language. The three best speech cues that worked are the following:

—"Show Mommy/Daddy."

If she was trying to tell us something and we didn't understand her, we'd tell her to show us. This led her to showing us how her toy broke or that there was a spider in the kitchen. (This worked until she learned how to sign *spider*. Then she'd show us where the spider was.) Once, she even went to get a fly swatter and showed that to us instead of telling us that there was some insect intruder in the home.

—"Point to it."

If Jennifer wanted something to eat, she'd sign *hungry* and we'd ask her to point to what she wanted to eat. Once she pointed at a box of cereal and another time she pointed at a can of soup. She understood what these things were and just by her pointing them out, we could tell exactly what she wanted. Later, with our second child, he'd point at the door, if someone was knocking, or at the smoke alarm, if it was going off.

—Asking.

The bathtub episode was just one way we used asking to communicate better. We'd also ask her if she was trying to tell us about something that happened, or if she was talking about a person? For example, when I *think* I know what she is talking about, I'll ask her something like, "Are you hungry?" or, "Did you see something?" Her answers help me to get a better idea of what she was talking about. One day as we played outside, she suddenly ran up to me, shaking. I asked her what was wrong, but had trouble lipreading her answer. I noticed she kept looking at the fence, and I asked, "Did you hear something?" She nodded, pointed at the fence then said, "Big truck." Sometimes, though, she wouldn't say outright what she was trying to say whenever we used this method. Sometimes she'd say, "No, I (blank)." We would get clues over the words we *did* understand her say through lipreading and sign, then work from there.

Sometimes, it was a matter of combining those three things. For example, she would show us something and we'd ask what she wanted. If she pointed at the DVD player, we'd ask if she wanted to watch a movie, then run through her favorite titles until we found the one she desired. Or she would show us her bed then point at something stuck on the side of it.

It took detective work, but using these methods helped us to communicate when the communication barriers cropped up a time or two. We would also tell her to tell another person what she was saying if we couldn't read her mumbling lips, and hope that person had better luck understanding her. It worked out okay, in the long run.

As she learned signs and her speech developed better (without all the mumbling!), we got to a point where we didn't have to use these methods anymore. During her toddler years, however, they were the communication methods that worked best when lipreading or sign language were not possible.

Deaf Culture and Deaf Parenting

Okay, so I am deaf now, I remember thinking shortly after I lost my hearing. I guess I'll have to learn sign language.

That idea didn't survive for very long. After I lost my hearing, my parents informed me that they were not interested in learning sign language to communicate with me. *We live in a hearing world*, they said. *You will learn how to read lips.*

That sort of task took a long time to learn. I soon found that some people, like my mother, were easier to lipread than others, like my father. If I couldn't lipread someone, my mom was usually asked to tell me what was being said.

However, it was not my mother who carried the burden of being the only one to communicate with this newly-deafened member of the family. Thankfully, two of my sisters took it upon themselves to learn how to fingerspell words to me, which seemed to be acceptable in my family. But using sign language? No.

I am not resentful of this *oral only* experience with my family. I am grateful they stressed the importance of being able to read lips, because as a deaf person I know it's important to be able to, but a part of me still longed for everything that was a part of the deaf community. Namely, using ASL. If my family had welcomed using sign language early on, I would not have struggled with it so much later or taken so long to learn it.

I was enrolled into a mainstream school that had a strong deaf presence. I found a sense of belonging among my deaf and hard-of-hearing peers. I still wore a hearing aid, but a lot of us communicated by sign. Still, as someone who came from an oral home, my use of sign was limited. My deaf friends seemed to understand this and started showing me certain signs. The ASL interpreters in the classroom accommodated my limited grasp of sign language by spelling things out or writing them down.

While submerged in that world which embraced ASL, I started to pick up on signs as well. Pretty soon, I was able to communicate with my deaf friends using sign.

One obstacle came about during this time, however: The limited use of my left hand. Many signs require two hands, and when I tried to use these signs with people asking what signs were for something, their imitation of how my left hand appeared while signing that word or words was not correct. It got to where I had to use my right hand for both the right and left hand signs. As an example, I'd say something like, "No, make the *P* sign with your left hand, too, like my right hand and just shake them both like this," for showing the sign for *play*. When that didn't work, I'd just use one hand or fingerspell the words.

Obstacle or no, I still tried to learn sign language, despite my parents' insistence I rely only on lipreading. I had nothing against lipreading, but as a deaf person, I wanted to know my language. Some argue that sign language is not a *language* per se, that it is only *signed supported English.* Yet telling a deaf person they cannot communicate by sign language at all is like telling a native of Germany they cannot speak German at all. This is our communication method for understanding each other and reaching out to each other, whether it is American Sign Language, British Sign Language, African Sign Language, or any other. Sign language is the language of the deaf. It is our language, and it is also the best way to get through to us when other communication methods fail.

That is, for those of us who know it.

Somehow or another, I got through those teen years knowing limited sign language. Then I learned about something called *Deaf Culture.* I had no idea what Deaf Culture was and what it meant, but after I started living on my own and was not bound to the restrictions of an oral only home, I started to learn more about this deaf community and Deaf Culture I was a part of.

Or was I?

According to the purists of Deaf Culture, assisted listening devices (ALDs) such as hearing aids and cochlear implants (CI) were shunned. These purists embraced and promoted *true* deafness.

At first, however, I didn't realize this opinion was limited only to the purists. It would be much later before I learned that it's perfectly fine to wear a hearing aid and still call yourself *deaf.*

Before that realization struck, however, I was stuck with an identity crisis. During the very early period as a new parent, I identified myself as *deaf.* But was I really deaf? I wore a hearing aid and it helped me *hear* a little. Maybe *hearing-impaired* was the right term.

With this idea, I started referring to myself as hearing-impaired.

As a hearing-impaired parent, I did appreciate having the hearing aid. It let me know when the baby was crying, when the washing machine was running and when there was a knock at the door. This provided a sort of *safety net* for me. Many times, I thanked my lucky stars for the hearing aid. As a parent, it just made life a little easier; I wasn't so terrified.

One thing I noticed, however, is that with a hearing aid, I relied on sound too much. When people spoke to me, I concentrated on what I could hear, and not what I could see or lipread. *This is not a good thing,* I often told myself, after once again asking someone to repeat what they said and *really* focusing on reading their lips. It got to a point where I'd match words I heard with the lip movement I saw.

Another disadvantage of having the hearing aid? I relied on it too much for everything else. I got lazy in keeping an eye on my child. I'd just listen for any noises, then turn around to check on her.

Meanwhile, I had what I'd learned about Deaf Culture reminding me that hearing aids are a Very Bad Thing. These disadvantages of wearing the hearing aid only reinforced that message. It was preventing me from being a good DEAF parent!

This led me to wonder, is this why purists of Deaf Culture refute wearing a hearing aid? Do they believe that such a device would hinder a deaf person from being able to thrive in the deaf world, while living in a world that is predominantly hearing? I had to wonder, and this theory made me take a good hard look at just what the hearing aid was doing for me as a deaf parent. Sure, it made life easier, but it was still hindering my survival strategies as a deaf person. To be honest, I felt helpless without a hearing aid! (It was only many years later when I was forced to go without a hearing aid that I was *comfortable in my own skin,* so to speak, and keep myself on top of things as far as surviving as a deaf person was concerned.)

Further reasoning on this theory had me look at my parents' refusal to learn sign language and try to understand why. Did they think that learning sign language meant I would stop being a part of the hearing world I'd lived in for 13 years? My mother, possibly aware of deaf people who mutely signed, was very worried that the next thing I'd lose was my voice. She constantly encouraged me to keep talking and, if I wasn't talking loud enough, to speak up. I was naturally a soft-spoken person—even in chorus at school, the music teachers complained they never heard me singing even though I *did* sing—so this confusion over keeping my voice going strong had me believing I *would* lose my voice next! To this day, I still speak softly, though when I do try to speak loudly, I end up getting a dirty look from some people, who think I'm shouting at them. Perhaps my parents thought using sign language would prompt me to talk less and less, just as the hearing aid led me to lipread less and less, though using sign language didn't threaten my ability to speak. Even after I used signs, I would say the things I was signing in front of them just to show using sign language didn't mean I'd stop talking. Unfortunately, by this time, it was years after I'd become deaf and I was getting a very late start in learning sign language.

The next thing that happened remains a mystery to this day. I developed an inner-ear rash that made wearing the hearing aid extremely painful. I had an inner-ear hearing aid, since it was the kind that worked best for me, and after the rash, I finally gave up wearing the hearing aid altogether.

The world of absolute silence I was thrown into after this happened left me petrified. I was not prepared for complete and utter deafness, even as I'd joke, "I really *am* as deaf as a post!" My husband and I tried to get different kinds of hearing aids, all to no avail. Each one only started that rash in my ear all over again. It was like my ear was physically rejecting a hearing aid! I couldn't help but wonder if this was a condition induced by my own psychological misgivings about wearing a hearing aid.

The one good thing that happened about losing the hearing aid is that I got back on track to being a good deaf parent. Now I was really a Deaf person! I was finally a part of Deaf Culture!

Still, one thing was missing: Sign language. Perhaps I'd become deaf in an oral home, and I started to notice how I tried to make my own home with my own children an oral home as well, but it wasn't long before I saw just how important it was to have sign language be a part of our home life. With a hearing child who has deaf parents, she should know the language used by the deaf and hard-of-hearing to communicate with each other, because we as a family would need sign language to communicate. It was not me saying, "We are only a deaf home," for my sake or. "We are only a hearing home," for the child's sake. It was me combining the two worlds. I made the decision to do something a little bit different than what my parents wanted in their home. I'd combine the Deaf world and the Hearing world. It would not be oral only or signing only. It would be both.

By exposing my child to sign language and letting her know what Deaf Culture is all about, I know she'll grow up with richer experiences she can carry with her when she goes out into the world. Both of my children will reap these benefits. They won't be clueless about sign language, as I was. They won't be unfamiliar with Deaf Culture, as I was. They will speak and sign, just as I speak and sign.

This kind of arrangement helped me make peace with Deaf Culture in my role as a deaf parent. I will expose my children to the deaf community, tell them all about groups like CODA (Children of Deaf Adults) and encourage their awareness of programs and schools for the deaf. Most of all, I'll make sign language a priority. Instead of choosing one over the other, we will choose both. We will speak and sign together. Because no matter what advocates of the deaf community say or ardent members of the hearing community suggest, it's ultimately our job to decide what part of both the deaf world and Deaf Culture we want to integrate into our lives. It has to be a personal choice.

As I learned later on, it's perfectly acceptable for me to wear a hearing aid and still be a part of the deaf community. A hearing aid is just a tool to help make life more enjoyable; it is not an object of shame. Even as some proponents of Deaf Culture shun hearing aids, I learned that other proponents have no qualms about wearing one. Many deaf people, people who do identify themselves as deaf and not hard of hearing, wear hearing aids, but they sign, too. They advocate rights for the deaf and tackle issues relating to the deaf community as a whole. A hearing aid doesn't make us any less a member of the deaf community any more than it would make a paraplegic any less a member of the disabled community simply for using a wheelchair.

Thanks to my experiences before I couldn't wear a hearing aid anymore, however, I have learned just how important it is to keep those survival strategies as a deaf parent in place. Moreover, keep the use of sign language in place. It is, after all, my language.

Being both hearing impaired and deaf helped me to see just where I stood in the deaf community. It helped me to understand and appreciate Deaf Culture better. Some things I take to heart, others I adapt to or revise as far as being a parent is concerned. Nothing is *one size fits all* for every parent, yet for something like sign language and embracing the deaf world, there is no harm in making these a part of the deaf parenting experience. I am deaf, whether or not I wear a hearing aid. Making those aspects of the deaf world just another part of the hearing world we as a family live in enriches our lives, strengthens our bond, and helps us as a deaf-and-hearing family grow together.

Silent Love

There are many things I have had to grapple with as a deaf parent: The fear of not hearing my child's cry for help, discrimination from the hearing world, and having to change everything the hearing world has told me about what parenting is all about since, as a deaf parent, I relate to it differently.

Any of these pitfalls can come and go. Any of them can vary in how they occur. And any one of them may someday disappear.

But there is one downside to being a deaf parent that took some time to adjust to: I will never get to hear my children say to me, "I love you."

My children hear me say those three words to them every day, but I will never get to hear those three words coming from them. Short of my hearing miraculously being restored, I won't ever hear my children's voices telling me that they love me. Perhaps my desire to have my hearing restored by some form of divine grace is a selfish one, given that there are so many other deaf parents out there coping with this same exact issue, but, the truth is, I would give *anything* to hear their voices.

We all want to hear somebody tell us that they love us. Somehow, hearing these words makes that love all the more strong. Nothing, not even chocolate, gives us the same sense of happiness and warm fuzzies inside the same way that hearing someone tell us they love us does. Hearing this from your own child does more than strengthen your bond; it's like a special, verbal gift. And that's a gift most parents wouldn't trade for anything. Ever.

As a deaf parent, I have pretty much accepted that I won't be able to hear things. When I was wearing a hearing aid during Jennifer's first months, I constantly marveled over the sound, though filtered, of her laughter. I couldn't get over how she would squeal with delight or make baby noises. I was even able to hear her cry. But without the hearing aid, I can only imagine what these sounds are like. It is just too different. My children's cries are muted and so are their voices.

I never heard my children's first words. As it is, I don't even know if the first word heard out of Jennifer's mouth was indeed her first. She could've been talking long before my dad told me one day she said *hi.* I've always wondered if that was her first word. I mean, babies usually say *Mama* or *Dada* first. But since I can't (and will never) know, it's just something I have to accept. That same acceptance happened after my second child was born; Jennifer told me Jesse's first word was *cut,* but how do I know it was his first? I don't, so I have to accept that the first word a hearing person caught was the first word my baby said. (As a side note, I can only wonder if Jesse's first word indicates a future in directing movies.)

This is just the way it is for me as a deaf parent. Other deaf parents out there probably have some other system in place to catch their child's first word. For me, the first word isn't really the first unless someone who can hear is with the baby 24/7.

But what about when it comes to catching when a child says, "I love you," to their parent? Relying on the ability to hear it is pointless as a deaf parent; relying on the ability to see it signed should take precedence. Still, for a long time, it panged me that I couldn't hear my child say *I love you* to me. I knew before I became a parent that I would never hear my children's voices. I knew this. I just never understood how hard and painful accepting this fact would be. A device exists to alert you to when your baby cries, but there is nothing to help you actually hear, with their real voice and not an amplified voice via a hearing aid, that your baby says *I love you,* not even on those days when *really* hearing it would help.

I am not alone in coping with this hard fact. I know some other deaf parents who have found this difficult to accept, too. One deaf parent said, "Does it bother me that I'll never hear my child tell me that he loves me? I can't let it."

This is a coping mechanism that I try to implement every day to move beyond the sadness and anger over never getting to hear, "I love you, Mommy."

But there are so many other ways my children and I get to express our love for each other, such as those moments of rocking them to sleep or when I take care of them. Each rock of the rocking chair is the two of us saying *I love you,* and knowing that sentiment is there. Each hug and kiss has that same affect. I will never hear my children tell me they love me, but I have to remind myself that actions speak louder than words. Love doesn't have to be spoken, in this case; it can be shown.

Sign language is how we *say* those three words to each other, and signing *I love you* has become just as effective as hearing it. The sign for *I love you* isn't one my children easily mastered at first, but they did manage to make something close to it with their small hands.

For Jennifer, it took some time for her to be able to sign *I love you.* At first, we used a home sign, one that was easier for her to make. I tried showing her the sign for *love* to replace the more difficult I love you sign, but something as simple as placing two arms over the chest as though hugging oneself was still hard for her to understand that this meant a sign of affection. When I signed *I love you* to her, that was how I showed my affection. When she made her own *I love you* sign back with her fingers, displaying something not even close to the real thing, I took this as her show of affection all the same. After she managed to sign *I love you* without trouble, she signed it all the time.

When Jesse was about a year and a half old, he also had trouble signing *I love you.* Instead, he said something that resembled *I love you* and pointed at me. In some way, this was his way of saying, "Right back at ya!" After he turned two, during the time his father was teaching him the game *Paper, Rock, Scissors,* where he'd hold his two fingers up for scissors instead of sideways, to make it look like he was signing peace, I still tried to gauge just how well he could sign *I love you.* I tested this by constantly signing it to him, he responded by making the sign for *peace,* and all of a sudden we became hippies.

Nevertheless, these efforts were just as good and all the more meaningful. Lipreading my children saying these words became a powerful substitute for hearing those words, as well.

And, anyway, they get the hang of signing *I love you* eventually. Later on, as Jesse got older, he was able to sign it without any trouble and now he signs it all the time.

Yes, it would be nice if I could hear my children say *I love you* to me, but I can't. It won't happen because I am deaf. I can't hear them say it, but I can *see* them say it. And that is almost the same thing.

Once, when Jennifer was younger, I learned just how powerful that could be. One evening, as Jennifer and I relaxed on the couches to watch TV, I turned to her and said, "I love you, baby." I watched her look at me, then lipread her saying, "I love you, too, Mommy."

I turned back around in the chair, a big smile on my face and my heart bursting with joy. Warm fuzzies flooded me from within and I was on top of the world. I may not have heard her tell me that she loves me, but, you know what? I didn't need to.

The Real Threat to Deaf Parents

Becoming a deaf parent means facing the same challenges any other parent will face: Lack of sleep, less time for myself, feeding routines, messy diapers, and so on. All of these things come with the territory, but they aren't a threat. There is also discrimination from the hearing world, but this isn't a threat, either. And, finally, there are the communication hurdles to work through. This, too, is not a threat.

What is a threat is the very real and very frightening chance that my child will be taken away from me.

One actual story of this happening, reported in an issue of *SIGNews,* stays with me. It is the story of Vicki and Eric Neuman, a deaf couple living in Wyoming. Their young son was taken from them because family members argued that they could not be good parents, mainly because they are deaf. The Neuman's story, though shocking, is unfortunately not too unusual. I have read of other cases in my research and normal Web-surfing of news stories. I've read of this happening in San Francisco, Canada and England. It is not just happening to the deaf parents, though; it also happens to parents who are deaf and blind. In some cases, the children are returned, but only under the provision that the authorities have the right to drop in every so often to monitor the child's well-being.

This is the way it is today, a sad reality for disabled parents who must tolerate discrimination. This is the very real threat that deaf parents everywhere face. I haven't had this happen to me (thank God!), but I'm aware of the possibility that it could. I am aware that the hearing world is watching me *very closely* to make sure I don't *neglect* my child in not watching her every minute or that I don't *abuse* her by forbidding a radio from the home. This is the shadow I live in every day, and I am not alone. Every other deaf parent in this world lives in this shadow, too.

My first child has survived for over ten years without authorities stepping in and she is doing *just fine.* She's a normal, active kid who plays with blocks, plays with her dollies, watches her favorite TV shows, dances to music, sings songs, colors pictures, reads books and has tea parties. She dresses herself, puts her toys away, speaks very clearly (according to my family), can recite the alphabet, sing nursery rhymes and eat with silverware. She has never been neglected, beaten or otherwise exposed to dangerous substances in the home (I don't allow smoking or drugs inside my home). We have a good, solid relationship, and I am there for her whenever she needs me.

Of course, all of this can never be enough to satisfy everyone. There is always going to be someone who will see me make a mistake then turn around and accuse me of being an unfit parent. This happens to deaf parents all the time. There's always that one little thing the hearing people will use against a deaf parent to assume the child is in a dangerous situation. They can't read the parent's minds. They may think a deaf parent doesn't realize the baby is crying, not laughing, as they try to play with the baby, whereas the deaf parent will *know* the baby is crying, but they are trying to cheer them up, anyway.

I feel there are certain things we, the deaf parents, must do to prevent the heartbreak of losing our children from ever taking place in our own home:

Deaf parents everywhere must educate, inform and empower themselves against the threat of having their children taken from them because of their deafness. There are deaf advocacy groups that can be found on the Internet, which will help deaf parents who have lost their children in such cases. The system is not always right—deaf parents have false accusations lodged against them and the accusers almost always win—but there are groups and laws in place to protect these parents' rights to care for their children. The groups are not always easy to find, and this is where a search on the Internet is helpful. Failing this, there's almost always a local disability assistance program or attorneys who assist the disabled to turn to.

I have to keep in mind that looks are everything. I must keep my home clean, my child's environment safe, and all medical supplies locked out of her reach.

I must not allow questionable people to watch over my child.

I must always keep my home drug-free.

I must always be consistent in keeping a close eye on my child.

I must find a way to communicate with my child—this is *very important.*

I must never say I can't do something because I am deaf or that this parenting stuff is too much for me because I am deaf.

I must stand up for my rights as a parent. Deaf or not, I *am* a parent first.

I must never lose my cool in public and never, ever let someone assume that, because I am deaf, they need to help me.

Another thing I must remember is to rely on my other senses, particularly smell, as much as possible. There was one time I knew Jennifer was standing behind me with a banana, mainly because I could smell the banana.

I must remember to use ALL of myself to move around, do things, juggle tasks, etc. Because of my left hand being the way it is, I have mostly relied on using my right hand to do everything. However, after taking a physical therapy session in which I was encouraged to use my left (bad) hand to complete tasks, I realized, I can do this! This made me realize how very little I actually use my left hand, only because I *thought* I couldn't use it. Since then I've remembered to use *both* hands to get jobs done, even when I think I don't need to. I'll even challenge myself to do things with my left hand just to accomplish doing that thing with that hand. If anything, including my left hand more often helps me to get the job done just a little bit faster.

I must remember the rule, *better to be safe than sorry.* I have to keep an eye out for a *possible* danger and ensure that danger has no way of happening. While some people have kept telling me things like *you need to chill* and *don't worry, she's fine,* I know I can't take that chance. I can't always assume everything is fine. My children are too important to me to take that chance! I can't let my children play alone for too long. I can't assume they'll be okay just because there's no danger now. I can't while away my days thinking everything will always work out perfectly. I won't let my children get too close to an opened window because the screen might loosen and someone could fall out. Or maybe my child will fall and get hurt if I let her jump on her bed. Maybe she'll choke on a piece of candy she's eating if I don't watch her while she's eating it. (There was actually one time Jennifer *almost* choked on a piece of candy! Then another time Jesse almost choked on his food. To this day I am grateful I was watching each child in each instance and paying attention to physical reactions.) The point is to avoid a possible danger. It really *is* better to be safe than sorry.

The above guidelines are not just good ideas I keep in mind to survive as a deaf parent, but they are also good ways for me to be more self-reliant. I know I can't do *everything* by myself (though life often makes me wonder otherwise!), but I really feel it's important to have that self-sufficiency in order to stay one step ahead as a disabled person.

If I need help, I know I must get that help from someone I trust—and that it is totally okay to ask for that help. I can't let a bad situation get worse. It's very hard for a first-time deaf parent to get through this parenting thing with their sanity intact. Every first-time parent freaks out at some point; it's normal. I know that if I need help, I must get that help from family or friends. I can't, for a minute, think that it's *too hard* to be a deaf parent. It is hard, but not *too* hard. And it's not impossible.

This doesn't mean that certain people realize that, too. Unfortunately, as ridiculous as it may sound, a lot of people still think a deaf person cannot be a good parent. That kind of thinking has been around for ages and it doesn't look like it'll disappear anytime soon. While deaf parents are faced with the threat of losing their children to people who think they know better, this doesn't mean that nothing can be done and rights can be violated. Civil rights are not contingent upon a person's abilities or lack thereof; a parent who loses their children simply because they are deaf has had their rights violated, just as a man who has been imprisoned simply for writing a letter protesting the government.

One day we will live without the threat of our children being removed from our homes, but until that day comes, deaf parents everywhere must stand up for their rights and for their children's rights to enjoy life together as a family.

The Socializing Stigma: Communicating with Hearing Parents

Brace yourself! They're coming! Headquarters has confirmed that they are on the move.

Hide your children!

Lock your doors!

Turn off all your lights and be prepared!

For we are about to be confronted with . . . Other. Children's. Parents.

You know, the ones that can hear.

Eeeek!

This is the kind of perception I had after Jennifer got older and wanted to play with other children and be at friends' houses. Aside from those other homes she'd be going to and other adults she'd meet, her dad and I are the only deaf adults she'd known. Now not only would she *safely* have other hearing children to play with outside of home, as she did at preschool where her teacher Kim was the only other hearing adult I communicated with, but she was pulling me, her deaf mother, right into this brand new world of hearing people. No more quietly, innocently isolating myself behind closed doors, comfortable in my deaf/hearing world that was free of discrimination or communication roadblocks. Now I had to get *out there* . . . and communicate with other hearing parents.

Oh, no! What if they see me as some kind of horrible parent just because I'm deaf? What if they think I'm too stupid to understand anything or that I get defensive about my deafness easily? These were the thoughts that ran through my head.

Even if these hearing parents did not have me under their watchful eye or become huge people staring down at little ol' me with their magnifying glasses, this was how it appeared to me before I had enough courage to meet with them.

My concerns over being accepted as a deaf person, and even as a deaf parent, were not the only concerns holding me back. I'm not a very sociable person. I *do* like being around people, and as a writer, I like just to watch people. But I don't throw myself into groups or die a little inside if I don't have people to hang out with every single day. I'm not so gregarious. I'm a lone wolf and prefer very few people around instead of a huge crowd.

On the Internet, it's different. I talk up a storm. I post on blogs, send out emails and participate on Facebook and Twitter. On the Internet, I am a *very* social person. But in real life, I don't start yakking my head off when I'm around people. I'm actually more private in real life.

So I had to wonder if my not being so talkative would come off as bizarre or just plain strange to other hearing adults. Worse, it might fuel the misconception many in the hearing community have that a deaf person cannot speak. I've been told by a hearing person that I speak so well, she would never have assumed I was deaf unless I told her.

As these worries tortured me, I knew I had to get past them and *just do it,* already. Meet the other children's parents, meet the hearing teachers and the other hearing adults my child comes into contact with. I *have* to meet them. I have to know them. I have to know the who, what, where, when, why and how of what's going on in my child's life—and the people involved in her life.

Like it or not, deaf or not, I realized I had to break through my isolation, get past my fears and worries, and socialize with hearing parents.

As it turned out, as I introduced myself to these parents and these adult figures in my child's life, and as I told them I am deaf, there was no discrimination from any of them. At all. Some were curious, some were delighted at finally knowing someone who is deaf (or someone else who is deaf, as many shared they had a deaf nephew or a deaf cousin), but none of them ran away screaming in terror. The common opinion among these hearing parents was this: "Oh, okay. You're deaf. Got it."

In fact, it ended up being the *children* of these hearing adults who were the most curious. Jennifer once shared with me the many questions kids at her school asked, such as *How do you and your mom talk to each other? How can she watch the TV? How does she know if you need help?* I went over this with her, explaining that kids will naturally be curious about something they don't understand, and that it's okay to ask questions. I asked her about how she answered these questions and cleared up any confusion she had about some questions she didn't have an answer for. For example, one child wanted to know why I am deaf, and I explained to Jennifer that she should say I got really sick with meningitis and that is why I lost my hearing. This led to a discussion of what meningitis is and why some people become deaf because of it.

Still, I had another roadblock to get through with these other hearing parents. Now that we all knew each other and it was understood that I need people to look at me when they speak, the next thing to go over was how to communicate. Whenever I meet a new person, I mentally judge the best way to communicate with them. If they don't know sign language or how to fingerspell, I try reading their lips. If that doesn't work, we try writing things down. Sometimes I could lipread most of what they said, but there were times I didn't get a word or part of a sentence and they had to write things down. The big challenge here was coming into contact with people who naturally talk too fast for me to lipread them or who have the habit of swinging their heads around or using gestures when they talk. If they are not comfortable writing things down, they usually had somebody else relay what they said. Conversations with these types of people predictably ended up coming to an end.

One other option to help out in communicating with other hearing adults was using cell phones. Specifically, texting on cell phones. One neighbor's son often typed out what he said on his cell phone if I wasn't able to lipread him, or sometimes he just saved us both the time and trouble and just showed up at my door with messages typed on his phone. A mom at one of Jennifer's basketball games started using her cell phone to type messages to me, and if she had my cell number, we could have just texted back and forth during the entire game. Texting has indeed been a godsend for me as a deaf parent, and not just for the times I couldn't understand what others were saying. It definitely came in handy when my deaf husband was at work when I went into labor with our second child.

As I have socialized with hearing parents, one thing I've noticed is the eternal attachment to the phone. For a hearing person, it's so easy for one person to say, "Yo! I'll call ya later!" and for the other to say, "Got it!" But for the deaf, there needs to be a little explaining done first. I'm all too happy to receive a phone call from someone, but first they must understand they'd have to use a relay service to call me. The person they end up speaking to won't be me, but a relay operator who will type to me what they say. I use online relay, with sites such as Sprint Relay or i711.com, and using relay means dialing the relay service number, not my home phone number. You give my home phone number to the relay operator. And after you finish what you have to say, you have to say, "Go ahead," to let the operator know it's my turn to *talk*.

Some hearing adults, not just hearing parents, I've shared this information with had no problem using relay. Many admitted it was *weird* and very different than what they're used to. In some cases, they ended up just saying, "I'll email you," because relay calls can take a little extra time on the phone and many used their cell phones as their main number, thereby complicating just how many minutes they'd have available for the call. This is completely understandable. The only irritant about this phone attachment is doctor's offices saying, "We can't send email," and not using relay to contact by phone. In situations like this, I have to say, "I will call back later," and get a time or a day to call. Relay, email or texting are all great ways for me to communicate with others when there's little or no in-person communication taking place.

And besides email, I have also used instant messaging to communicate with others. Once upon a time, I was on America Online (AOL), but after that ended, I started using Yahoo! Messenger or Google Talk. So chatting online is another way to communicate with the hearing parents, as well, though I have not yet chatted regularly with any hearing parents. Just hearing people.

It's been quite a journey in communicating with other hearing parents and adults as my children grow and are exposed to more people in their lifetime. I am grateful I tore down those walls of isolation and got out there to network with them, because knowing so many of them has enriched my life, just as it has for my children. And actually, socializing with them hasn't invaded my privacy and we're not suffocating each other, so I still get lots of time to myself, as well.

Sometimes, a situation like this is just a matter of finding the communication method that works best—sign language, lipreading, writing or texting—and other times it's just a matter of sitting down to look at one another and speak slowly and clearly enough to have a regular conversation. I rarely have to remind them to look at me when they speak, and only once has a person taken issue with me about being deaf and unable to communicate like a *normal* person.

That's the best part of this experience so far. There is such a widespread acceptance of the fact that I'm deaf. Granted, we can't live under the impression that the hearing world is clueless about the fact that there are deaf people which they share this world with, but because of discrimination and misconceptions about the deaf, reaching out and socializing with the hearing community is a journey we must take on slowly and with caution. Once we establish that discrimination and those misconceptions are not there, it's easier to act like two regular people just trying to get to know each other and communicate with each other like two regular people are supposed to do.

A Bridge between Worlds: Deaf Parent, Hearing Child

There is a memory from Jennifer's toddler years that I like to recall: Jennifer sitting in the bathtub, giddy with anticipation and me holding my breath as I watched her hands circle the plastic cup. Slowly, she presses the sides of the cup together, turning its circular mouth into an oval. Her hands move away and we both watch as the cup *pops* out again. Both of us laugh every time that happens, even though she's laughing at the noise the cup makes when it pops and I'm laughing over the surprise. I like to remember this because it reminds me of a time when we found a common way to appreciate something as a hearing person and a deaf person. In so many other ways, we find common ground in the two worlds we share in our home: The deaf world and the hearing world.

As a deaf parent, I may never be able to be surprised by noises or unexpected sounds the same as my hearing children can, but at the same time, I can laugh or act surprised with them, simply for the sake of being surprised. In the same way, the children experience my deaf world through watching a television program with closed-captioning or using their hands and body language to communicate.

When there is a deaf parent with a hearing child, the parent lives in two worlds every day: the deaf world and the hearing world. The child enjoys sound while the parent can't, yet technology and simple actions still allow the parent to be a part of these experiences in some way. The parent uses sign language to communicate while the child uses her voice, but she can learn how to sign in order to communicate.

When we once played a game I created called *Where's the Baby?* in which Jennifer or her little brother will hide under a blanket as I call out, "Where's the baby?" and we laugh and tickle after they pop out from under the blanket as I announce, "There's the baby!" then this is something that is a part of the child's hearing world. When we go to the doctor and the children see an interpreter signing to me, this is a part of my deaf world which they get to be a part of. These worlds, though very different, are still merged in our daily lives and it is this merging that helps us draw closer to each other in our own ways.

Events and methods like the ones mentioned above bridge these worlds. In some ways, I am different from my child. But in others, I am not. We're still bonded to each other in finding a way to communicate, live, play and learn.

And we still bond through love and nurturing.

Before I became a parent, it was only the *deaf world* I lived in with my future husband. After a hearing child entered the picture, with my knowing she must be able to enjoy the same things that are a part of every hearing child's life, the hearing world became part of our lives as well. I no longer lived in the *deaf world;* I lived in the *deaf/ hearing world* because it was where my children lived, too. Now instead of mutely watching a movie, I have to remember to turn the sound on if it's a movie my children can also enjoy. Instead of loudly tapping my foot on the floor when I'm writing, I have to remember that my hearing child is busy doing her homework, and the noise is a distraction. These combined worlds helped me to remember and appreciate the hearing people living in our home, while the hearing people learned to understand and appreciate the deaf people living in their home.

My deaf world teaches the children a wide variety of ways for them to communicate and interact with others. They can learn sign language and therefore grow up in a bilingual home because they'll end up being proficient in two languages. They can watch a movie with captioning and improve their reading and vocabulary skills, thanks to those words on the screen. On top of this, they may even be so inclined to mute the volume on the television set and watch a captioned television program without sound, just to see what it's like for Mom and Dad. They can learn how body language contributes to the way we speak, think and feel, as well as practice respectfully communicating with others by looking at them when they talk, and speaking clearly. I have noticed how a lot of hearing people are not attuned to these benefits and, because my children have deaf parents, they are in a position to be exposed to these manners of communicating with others and understand the importance of using them in their lives. Having a deaf parent puts the children into the position of understanding just how much a person's life changes once that ability to hear is gone.

In the same way, I have so much to learn and enjoy from my children's hearing world. Because I have hearing children in my home, I have to remind myself constantly to focus on the tone of voice I am using when I speak to them. This has been a big challenge for me, because I don't know how soft or loud my voice is when I talk, but it has definitely made me more aware of my tone of voice. If I'm sad, I try to sound sad. If I'm happy, I try to make myself sound happy by varying my tone. There are times the children may pick up on the wrong tone of my voice and react accordingly (or not react at all), and so it becomes something I try to improve on. Sometimes, for example, I think I'm speaking loudly when I'm being told not to yell. Other times, when I do something like move dishes around in the sink thinking I'm doing so quietly, I get a tug on my shirt and a reminder not to make so much noise.

Another benefit of living in these two worlds is that it helps me, as a deaf person, understand and remember just how important sound is to my children. Sound offers them enjoyment, satisfaction, diversions and instruction. Sound teaches them something new or encourages them to dance and sing. My husband always worries when the children play music, because he doesn't want it to be too loud and therefore invite complaints from our neighbors. I just shrug off the worries and let my children sing if they want to sing and dance if they want to dance. For this reason, I always try to keep sound in the home and I get to enjoy the sight when my children dance their hearts out to music or react with a facial expression from the sounds they hear.

These episodes get me to think about how I would react to such noise, and how, once upon a time, I used to enjoy doing things like that when I lived in the hearing world, too. I can no longer remember what it's like to be moved or excited by sound. I can't remember the feelings I'd get from listening to music or from the tone of a person's voice. But with my children, I get to experience these feelings and emotions again, even if it's just from watching them relive those moments.

With hearing children under the roof, I can no longer have a deaf only home. This is something which I struggled with at first, because I couldn't see how the two worlds could balance and thrive, but in time we have both grown to appreciate this combination. Just as my children are exposed to what life is like for the deaf, we, their deaf parents, are reminded of the hearing world they live in. By remembering to be aware of all of the highs and lows of the hearing world, how hearing can be taken for granted or how differently people can respond to what they hear, we see how this nurtures and shapes the lives of our children who themselves are trying to balance the two. Every day we live with our hearing children means we have to be a part of their hearing world by any means possible, because even if it's *their* world, it's one they still need us in.

The hearing world and the deaf world can coexist in a family, but it takes time and effort to find balance between the two. It takes patience and understanding, adaptation and consistency. I knew nothing about any of this before my children came along, except that it wasn't going to be easy being a deaf parent with a hearing child.

With time, though, things can work out to benefit both the deaf parent and the hearing children.

As my hearing children grow up living with deaf parents, we find a way to make the hearing world and the deaf world coexist without trouble in our home. We build that bridge between the two worlds by finding common ground and appreciating how things are different, and how they can be the same. At the same time, no matter what is different between one world that we share with the other, there is still a third permanent world which we will draw our strength from during this lifetime: The one world we have created that's called *Family.*

PART THREE:

Parenting Pauses

Words Real, Imagined and Silent

Jennifer sat in my lap while I was writing at the desk. Her box of crayons sat opened next to the two notebooks she'd been drawing in and her various other drawings rested on the far edge of the desk. She turned to look at me, holding up a crayon.

I looked at her and announce the color. "Green!"

"Yeah, green," she replied. "I'm going to draw a big house."

"A big house?"

"Yeah, a big house," she repeated, using her hands to illustrate just how big this house of hers was going to be.

I smiled and watched her turn back around to draw what only could be the artistic renderings of how a three-year-old thinks a *big house* should look. Mentally, I was feeling pretty good over having understood every word she just said, while at the same time I thought about how this isn't always the norm.

On some days, when she was that young, I didn't understand her every word. And on other days, I couldn't understand *anything* she said at all. But we still managed those turbulent toddler years when she didn't have a very broad vocabulary, expert grasp of how to use sign language and little understanding of the importance of looking at her deaf mother when she spoke.

Just as many deaf and hard-of-hearing people will bluff their way through a conversation, there have been many times I've done the same thing with my children. Some words I got, some words I didn't. There was one time Jennifer got frustrated I misunderstood a request she made. One day, she asked for what I thought were *cans*. When I brought her canned goods from the cupboard, which I thought she wanted to play with, she stomped her foot with an angry look on her face and said, "I said I wanted *crayons*, not cans."

This is a coping strategy I've adopted as part of being a deaf parent. It hasn't always worked out well and sometimes I have felt guilty for trying to bluff my way through a conversation with my children. As a parent, and especially as a deafened parent, I should get every single word that's being said to me, right? I should know *exactly* what is being said.

Well, not always. I never let on that I try to bluff my way through conversations with my children, but I think they do catch on that I'm not paying 100% attention to what was being said. I hate to admit that I don't make it an effort to understand *every single word* my children say to me. My children most often speak without signing, so I've gotten used to missing a word here or there. Sometimes I'll get it if they repeat what they just said, but other times, I won't.

And sometimes I'll be too distracted by something, have too strong of a headache to concentrate too hard on understanding them or be too caught up thinking about what I'm writing to get everything they say to me.

But at least nobody gets hurt and nobody suffers.

If I *do* need to know every single word that was just said to me, I'll say something like, "Jennifer, I want you to tell me one more time what you just said, and this time, please speak slowly and very clearly."

Sometimes I'm able to pick up exactly *every word* my children say, because they normally say the same thing in certain instances. For example, Jennifer's statement, "He's my friend," is reserved for the dog, and, "Silly Grandpa," was for when she saw a picture of my dad acting funny when he was dressed up as a rock star at a costume party on Halloween. And then there were the times Jennifer will repeat something I say, like whenever I sigh, "Give me a break!" (Have to be careful with that repeating stuff . . .). What's interesting is that, on many occasions, I can understand Jennifer better than other people, including hearing people, with the help of lipreading. With Jesse, the predictability applied even when he was a baby. Instead of saying *dog-dog* or *doggie* every time he saw the dog, I knew he was just saying *dog.* And when he put his hand against his right cheek and made a look of alarm, I knew he was saying *oh, no!* because he got that reaction from me.

Then it's just a matter of understanding how the children talk. Jennifer very rarely says *yes* (I've been told!), and once I've been clued in that she says things like *nice work* or *for me?* then I'm able to lipread those words, knowing it's exactly what she said. She's also prone to say the same thing every time something happens (like she'll say, "I've got hiccups," then, "Hiccups are gone," when she stops hiccuping) and she'll even say the same things I do in certain instances (like the first time we made a popping sound with her cup in the bathtub, I said, "It popped!" and then she'd say, "It popped!" every subsequent time she did this). She also called her books *stories,* and her dolls *babies.* Later, she started calling all of her stuffed animals her *babies.*

What's interesting is that, on a deeper level, I just *know* what my children are saying. No lipreading or signing happens during this occasion; it's like *parental instinct.* I suspect that, once a deaf person has known another person long enough and interacted with them enough times, they get into a sort of rhythm where they can understand each other without lipreading or signing. I guess this is a part of getting familiar with the speaking habits, as mentioned above, but I still find the whole process intriguing. It's like my mental ears pick up on what she is saying. (The same thing happens between me and her father. Sometimes, we don't even need to speak or sign to communicate. We just *know* what the other is saying or going to say.)

Of course, there are times I'll think Jennifer has said something when she didn't. This has happened before. I'll think she says one thing, but her dad lipreads another. Or one of my sisters or my mom will tell me she actually said something else. This has also happens when I try to get her to repeat the alphabet. I will ask her to sing the song and I'll go nuts when she's done, telling everyone, "She sang the whole alphabet!" Though her father thought I only *thought* she did because I wanted her to learn it so much. I admit, when she said *V* it looked like *B*. Who knows? When in doubt, I elected to have her sing the alphabet song in front of someone who could hear.

When I bluff my way through trying to communicate with my children when they don't sign, the feelings of guilt and worry are hard to push aside. Bluffing my way through a conversation with hubby doesn't cause guilt, and the same goes when I bluff with everybody else. People at the store, the ladies at the bank, the school officials. Sometimes I catch everything being said to me, sometimes I don't. And sometimes I'm too tired to pay complete attention to everything being said to me so that I can lipread it all and understand it all. Just as I will occasionally be too tired to get every single word my child says.

Still, with the children, that's where the guilt shows up if I try to bluff with them.

I feel guilty for not getting their every word, and guilty for not encouraging them to sign more. The worry comes up because I start to think that maybe she'll assume I don't think what she has to say is very important to me or that I might miss something I really should *not* miss.

Missing something very important my child has said has indeed happened a time or two. When it did, I ended up saying something like, "Jennifer, I didn't understand you when you asked me if you could do that. The answer is no." What followed in a situation such as this was her reluctant acceptance of this misunderstanding and my answer to her question. This kind of misunderstanding happens so many times between her father and me, usually because of bluffing, and it has caused many arguments or angry feelings between the two of us before the situation is finally set straight. But we don't make it a huge issue between us, because we both quietly accept that this is life for the deaf. And when it happens with my oldest child, she sees this as just one other thing that happens when having a deaf parent and it's not cause for some crisis.

Later, as my children started using sign language more often and we were able to communicate better, there wasn't really a need to bluff my way through a conversation anymore. Sometimes those slip-ups can cause a humorous result, sometimes they incite feelings of frustration or a need to be more patient. Whatever they bring out of the experience, the main thing I hope my children understand someday is that I only bluffed my way through a conversation with them because it seemed to be a good idea at the time. As a long-term method of communication, however, there is too much at stake to let it be the only way for me to get through communication hurdles. I don't need to hang on to every single word my children say, especially when they go on and on about their favorite TV show that I have no interest in, but I do need to know most of the things they are saying. After all, if it's worth their efforts to communicate those words to me, it's worth my efforts to understand those words. Every single one of them.

Run that Bleep By Me Again?

As Jennifer walked through the living room, my mother and I watching her as she moved, she fell to the floor and said something. My mother started laughing, swinging her head back and covering her mouth as her eyes widened. She shook her head, utterly amused.

"What's so funny?" I asked, looking at both my mom and my toddler.

My mother finally regained control of herself and looked at me. "She said *oh, s***.*"

My jaw dropped and I froze. She swore? She really just swore? Did that really just happen?

Admittedly, I have been known to say the occasional swear word. Okay, okay; I've said swear words a lot of times. I will admit it! But on that day, I hadn't said that word at all. And at the age of three, how was it possible for her to have remembered ever hearing that word?

This was just one more reminder that I have a *hearing* child in my home. Living with a deaf husband, we could say any old thing we wanted to, alone or with each other, and give little thought to it. Now, with a hearing child in our home, there were going to be tender ears hearing every single word her parents said.

After this incident, I tried to be more careful about my language, especially when I was within her earshot. I even tried to coax my husband into watching his language around our daughter, as well, but he would have none of it. His language remained just as colorful as a rainbow in the sky. He was convinced saying bad words around our young child wouldn't lead her to repeating them. After all, she was so young.

Then, one day, after I gave both of them a bowl of soup for lunch, we discovered otherwise. My husband irritably held up the tablespoon I'd given him and said, "I don't want this f****** spoon."

Ever the great imitator, our daughter likewise held up her spoon and said, "This f****** spoon!"

I stood there looking at her, my mouth agape. Did I just lipread her correctly? Part of me swore she said something like *fix this spoon,* which would make sense because she refused to use the spoon I'd given her just as her dad refused his, but another part of me noticed a word before the *F* word she'd said. That word was likely *this* but *this fix spoon* doesn't sound right and she was old enough to put her sentences together properly.

Growing up, I was not allowed to swear. However, like all young children, my siblings and I often whispered swear words among each other, giggling and thinking our parents couldn't hear us. We even set each other up accidentally to say a swear word, just to get each other into trouble. Still, even in secrecy, our parents occasionally caught us swearing. On one occasion, my father cornered my older sister and me about our swearing, though he was mainly mad at me because I was the one he heard swearing. During his interrogation, he asked me, "Do I swear?"

I wanted to say *Uh, yeah, Dad, you* do *swear a time or two.* Because that was the truth. But, instead, I had to lie. That wasn't the answer he wanted to hear, because I knew he was trying to make a point. So instead I told him what he wanted to hear. "No."

"You're damn right I don't," he said.

My sister and I secretly exchanged grins, saying between ourselves *there he goes again!*

It's true, my father did swear a lot. He seemed to have no qualms saying swear words when he spoke to us, such as the time he got angry at me for having romantic attachments to a man a few years older than I and how he yelled, "Use your damn brain, Dawn!"

Swear words were a part of my parents' vocabulary, just as any of the other words they used. They used swear words in casual conversations, though my father used them more often than my mother. And as history repeats itself, my husband swears more than I do. He'll say, "I don't give a s***," to me in front of the children, just as he would tell us where he was going before heading out the door.

I suspect I started swearing so much after I left home as a way to *rebel* against my parents' restrictions against swearing. I was untouchable now! I could swear away and not get smacked for it! Freedom!

It even got to where I started to take pride in my freedom to swear. At one point, when I took an online survey and was asked, "Do you swear?" I proudly answered, "Like a sailor!"

After my child started repeating those swear words, however, that pride took a nosedive. I started to take notice of my potty mouth . . . and how it was causing my hearing child to develop her own potty mouth because of it. Later, Jesse started repeating swear words, too.

Believe me, I tried everything to curb the swearing. Yet as I said things like, "I hurt my darn hand!" and, "This stupid computer!" (which is actually a common thing I like to say!), I started to feel like I was in Mayberry, or something. I'd adopt an emphasized country accent and say things like *gee whiz!* and *golly gee,* just to poke fun at my attempts to make my language more G-rated. After I got over this embarrassment, I tried to make up silly words in place of swear words. For the *F* word, I'd say *fook.* For the *B* word, I'd say *boatch.*

Or sometimes I'd say *shite, damnation, Hades* and *arse,* or even *derriere,* in place of the other words.

This wordplay was fun while it lasted, but the major times I swore were when I was hurt or angry. My emotions came over me and, you guessed it, those bad words started rolling right out of my mouth again. Just as Yosemite Sam releases a stream of expletives during his long falls in the cartoons, I've been known to do the same after getting angry or getting hurt. Screaming the words into a pillow helped, but my little ones were there to see and hear it all.

I tried using the *swear bucket* method, which I got the idea to use after noticing a friend's mom was using one, where a quarter was deposited into a can anytime somebody swore. I ended up with more words in my vocal bank than I had quarters in my pocket. I went into serious overdraft on my swear bucket account and that idea was eventually deep-sixed.

At this point, I just threw up my arms and gave up. I released the verbal hounds and pretty soon, Jennifer was once again saying the exact same bad words she heard at home. Wow, I was being such a *model* parent!

During her toddler years, I didn't always catch her saying a swear word. It was hard enough to lipread every other word she said; trying to lipread her when she was saying a swear word took effort. And repetition. I actually had to watch carefully as she spoke and keep an eye out for anything that looked like a swear word. When this happened, I had her repeat what she just said. The whole thing seemed ironic at first, asking a child to repeat, once or twice, a word they are *not* allowed to say, just to see if they did indeed say that word. I even ended up getting strange looks from people just because of this. But after I established that she had actually said the word, that's when I had to do something more proactive about it. But later on, as she grew older, she'd say she said one thing when I could've sworn she said something else.

I have explained to Jennifer she shouldn't say those bad words, because they are not proper language for a child, yet it still hung over her head that her parents swore up a storm. Why couldn't she?

I realize I could've just signed the words instead of saying them, yet I started to feel uncomfortable about Jennifer signing them in public, too. I don't know why it never registered with me that it was better to sign swear words than to say them, since it was the hearing community who might think I was letting my child run her mouth at everybody without caring enough to stop it. But I still thought signing the words might be more harmful than her hearing us say them. First of all, she'd just know they were bad words and might try getting away with signing a bad word at school, where her teacher might not know what that sign means and think she's just being silly. Second, the signs might be taken out of context. I could just see it all now: Jennifer going up to her BFF and, while making the sign for the *B* word, asking, "What does this sign mean?" Then her friend would tell her, saying the exact word it meant, and Jennifer would get all upset and defensive, demanding of her friend, "What did you just call me?"

Later, Jennifer became the Swearing Police, reprimanding me with, "You said a cuss word!" anytime she heard me utter such a thing. This was something I grew extremely grateful for. She *knew* those words were bad to say and she also knew she had to put her foot down about it being said in her presence.

As she started to take issue with my swearing, I started to develop a better method of watching my language. I started to *think* the words I wanted to say instead of actually saying them. This began after my husband and I got into several arguments and I ended up not correcting him about something with my voice but mentally correcting him instead. I carried that over into the moments where I got hurt and wanted to say the *S* word or when I got angry and wanted to say the *F* word. If I couldn't keep quiet, I'd let loose a scream instead.

At least a scream is much better for my children to repeat.

Do You Hear What I Don't Hear?

Music was blaring in the house. A two-year-old little girl was on the floor, covering her ears and crumbled into a ball as her mother sang at the top of her lungs: "O, CHRISTMAS TREE! O, CHRISTMAS TREE!!! BLAH, BLAH, BLAH, BLAH, BLAH, BLAH, BLAH!!!!"

It didn't matter that this particular mother couldn't remember all the words to that particular Christmas carol. Or that she just *might* be a teensy, tiny bit off in singing along with the song she had blasting from the TV music channel. Or even that she couldn't hear the song playing at all. All that mattered to this mother is that she was celebrating Christmas in one way she had always enjoyed as a child: Singing Christmas carols.

It's not just the Christmas season that allows me to relive the joy of singing Christmas carols. I love to sing, period. Even though I got kicked out of a Christmas performance in middle school and have been told I'm not much of a crooner, I sing, anyway. I have always sung, since childhood. Even after I lost my hearing at the age of 13, I continued to sing even, though I couldn't hear my own voice. And someday I hope to sing in public again.

I know it's odd for someone who is deaf to love music so much. I am very grateful that I had the blessing of knowing music before I could no longer hear it. Everyone in my family loves music.

We grew up playing music, dancing to it and singing along with it. Long car rides had my sisters and me belting out our favorite tunes. Perhaps this is why I don't think I'll ever stop loving music. It is very powerful and good for the soul. So is singing that music.

Nowadays, though, I only sing for my children. Sometimes, I've sung just because I wanted to, and those occasions happened when I was alone—or thought I was alone. Then I'd sing a tune in my head without actually using my voice, which felt safer for me to do. Yet for the most part, I sing for the children. There are many times I've rocked them to sleep singing lullabies and sometimes we even sing during baths. I have sung to my children since their births—even before they were born. I sang to them while they were in the womb and as I held them in the hospital room. I have sung to them every Christmas, rocking them to sleep to *Silent Night* or getting into a clapping spree as I belted out, "JINGLE BELLS, JINGLE BELLS, JINGLE ALL THE WAAAY!!!!"

My children love music, especially to dance to, so they have fun dancing along to music and even trying to sing along with me (thus why I have had to start singing a little slower every time I sing *Twinkle, Twinkle, Little Star).*

One thing about Christmas, though, is that it just would not be complete without Christmas carols. I have left the *Sounds of the Season* music channel on the TV for most of the day and Jennifer loved to dance to tunes like *Here Comes Santa Claus* and *Rudolph the Red-Nosed Reindeer.*

The thing about Christmas carols is that they can be enjoyed by everyone, whether they can hear, can't hear; can see or can't see. Even if they can't talk or move around so freely. Christmas carols inspire memories of Christmases spent with family, good times with friends, and embracing the season of giving and happiness. They inspire hope, reignite faith and help calm the stresses of daily life.

Best of all, they can be appreciated and enjoyed in so many languages, in so many parts of the world.

Because I want music to be a part of my children's lives so that they can enjoy it just as I once did, I remember to include Christmas carols every time the Christmas season rolls around. I'm pretty much limited to singing the songs I grew up with. *Silent Night, Rudolph the Red-Nosed Reindeer, Jingle Bells, O Christmas Tree,* and others. I can remember how most of them go, and this is where the Internet helps: I can look up the lyrics of popular Christmas songs so that the kids and I can sing them. As far as playing the songs goes, that really depends on if I can find them on a CD. When a song I know starts to play, that's when the spirits soar and my singing voice is set free.

Because even if my ears can't hear the songs, my heart still hears them. My heart remembers them, and it is from the heart where the spirit of Christmas and Christmas caroling can grow.

Adventures in Reading (and Signing)

A common piece of advice given to parents: Read to your children. That's a message I've taken as gospel and read to my children whenever I can. But because the parent in this case is deaf, and the children in this case are hearing, story time takes on a whole new adventure.

As a child, story time was different for Jennifer. It was like the rest of the world was gone. It's only the two of us, exploring a world or just having fun with words. While I could not hear her repeat the words that I said during these times, it was still a bonding experience.

The common message behind reading to or with our children is that it should be an educational experience. It should be a time where the child can understand and pronounce new and longer words. Some other suggestions recommended by experts are to allow the child to participate in the storytelling by asking them to share their own ideas and to see exactly which words the child can and cannot read.

Listening to my children's ability to read certain words or pronounce them correctly just isn't a task that can be done for me. But this doesn't mean story time is no longer an educational experience for them; it is. It also turns into a fun experience.

Because I can speak, I use sound effects as I read to my children. When I say that a bus is going through town, I'll make driving noises and pretend I'm steering the wheel. If I say the wind is blowing hard, I'll make exaggerated wind sounds. Sometimes, Jennifer imitated the sound effects I made. I didn't know this by sound, of course, but by lipreading her and watching the expression she made.

Lipreading is a big part of what I experience during my children's story time. Jennifer often grabbed the book to take over the reading and sometimes I didn't see her lips to tell if she was reading the words correctly, but more often than not, lipreading her has clued me in to what she said. Sometimes, she repeated a sentence or asked a question, and that's when we stopped reading the book to explore what she understood so far. Asking her if she understood the story can happen at any other time, though; sometimes, if I think she's confused, we'll linger over the pages, talking about what I just read. I'll ask her questions like, "Do you think the bunny is lost?" or I'll say simpler statements like, "He can't find his mommy."

Story time is also a great opportunity to teach my children the sign for something. If a picture in a book has simple objects, I'll point to them, then show the children the sign for it. For example, if there is a cup, I will point at it, say *cup* then make the sign as I again say *cup.* We sign *Mommy* and *Daddy* for the appropriate images, and I'll even try to squeeze in a signed sentence or two (as long as the sentences are simple, such as, "It started to rain.").

Most of the time, these signing lessons aren't always imitated on every try. There were times Jennifer watched me sign something then just turn the page. I still think nothing is lost. I think that on some level, and with enough repetition, they will catch on to the sign for certain objects. After all, once the story ends, we almost always turn back to different pages and I can sign things to them again. I'll know that extra effort has paid off after they sign those words back to me.

After we finish reading a book, we top the session off with a little discussion about the story. I will try to sign things again, but the main goal here is to see if they understood what we just read and if they can remember things. I will ask them something like, "Do you remember when the bunny was being naughty?" or, "Did the raccoon eat the nuts?" They won't always sign to me during this time, and they may not sign a single word, but as long as I can lipread them and get a straight answer, I let the lack of signing pass.

I don't try to make using (and learning) sign language a major part of our story time. Not yet, anyway. Once the children are older, sign language will be a bigger part of our story time, and it may even allow us to create alternative storylines or endings for our fictional friends.

Meanwhile, all that matters is that story time is still a fun and educational time for all of us to strengthen that parent-child bond in a deaf and hearing way.

Teaching Baby to Sign

A curious face looked up at me, staring in wonder. The eyes moved as she watched me try to show her a sign. I repeated my efforts, once again ending each presentation with the word I was trying to teach her the sign for, and all the while, she could only stare as though she was asking, *What's that thing you're doing with your hands, Mom?*

When she was an infant, I tried to teach Jennifer how to sign. After I learned that you can teach a baby as young as three months basic signs in sign language, I tried to show her various signs. Things, like: *Mommy, Daddy, sleep* and *play.* These attempts were all lost on her as she only stared in wonder at my hand making signs. Eventually, she tried to sign to us, as well, but all she could manage to do was move her fingers up and down.

This was a good sign, right? The effort was there. That's what I thought, so I kept at it.

One thing I decided to try, in order to make learning sign language easier for her, was to have a *word of the day* I'd sign to her. Each time this word was used, I'd sign it as I said it. I had to make sure the word of the day was one we'd commonly use, like *cup* or *book,* just so I could try to sign the word to her as often as possible. I figured that, with this approach, something would stick.

Unfortunately, my patience ran out. Three days and zero success later, that idea was deep-sixed. The signs just seemed to fly right over my toddler's head.

An article I read on teaching a baby sign language suggested that you go through your day signing everything you said. Make sure the baby sees you signing and speak as clearly as possible as you talk and sign, the article instructed. Because of my experience living in an oral home, I was still not as fluent in ASL as I wanted to be, so signing everything was not doable. Still, I gave this tactic a shot, signing everything I knew the sign for. Meanwhile, when she napped or I had some *me time,* I'd try to learn the signs I didn't know, just so they could become a part of our signing vocabulary. Even still, as an oral person, I was not used to signing as I spoke, so this method failed as well. I often forgot to sign as I spoke and I just dropped this strategy altogether. After all, I didn't know all the signs!

Maybe one of the methods I tried was the correct one and I just didn't give it enough time to work. I really don't know what *enough* time means but, looking back, I saw how I just didn't pursue these options long enough to have any lasting effect. A few days just wasn't enough time. As with potty training and bedtime, I had to be consistent.

Another guilty feeling that tugged at me was how I didn't try to teach Jennifer sign language early enough. Perhaps if I had started when she was three months old, and kept at it, she'd be fluent in sign language before she even said her first word. Or, maybe I should have consulted with some expert to find the best way to teach my baby how to sign.

Yet I saw those clumsy fingers and thought it was a lost cause. I noticed her confusion and thought it was too hard for her to understand that this was just another method of communicating with people, and why she needed to use this to communicate with us.

Added to this was how I didn't seek any outside support on how to teach my baby to sign. I didn't consult with family or friends. What book I did buy to try to teach her to sign didn't offer as much on instruction as it did entertainment.

As Jennifer got older and she was able to use her hands better, I started to try teaching her sign language again. This time, however, I started with the basics: The alphabet. Just as the first signs I learned were the signs for letters, so, too, would they be my daughter's first signs. When I was teaching her the alphabet by singing the alphabet song to her, I would slow down the song and pause with each letter, just long enough for her to see the signs for these letters. In this way, I hoped she would make the connection that this particular sign meant this particular letter. After several tries, and several days, I am proud to add, she finally started to copy the signs. At the same time she learned her letters, she learned the signs for them, too. Hooray! A breakthrough!

From there, I tried to show her other signs. I'd point at myself and sign *Mommy.* Then I pointed at her father and signed *Daddy.* She started to pick up on these signs and, from there, we moved on to others. *Water. Grandma. Grandpa. Book. Apple. Hot* and *home.* One thing I noticed is that Jennifer had different names for things. She called books *stories,* a stuffed animal was a *baby* and a cup was *drink*. I'd use these words while making the sign for them, just so she could understand what I was referring to.

My second child was the same way as a toddler. He calls food *yummy,* so we had to say *yummy* when signing food, just so he could understand what we were signing to him.

One thing my second child proved, however, is that not all babies don't have trouble signing just because their hands are not so flexible. Before he was two years old, Jesse was able to sign things like *more* and *all done.* Some signs are actually not all that challenging for small babies to learn. *More,* for example, only requires that a baby touch his fingers together then tap those closed fingers together. With the sign *Mommy,* all the baby needs to do is hold out their hand and touch the thumb to their chin. On the other hand, while Jennifer had trouble using her small hands to make signs, she also had to take some time to understand just what all this signing business was all about. Jesse learned signs faster, as though he *got it* that it was just another way to communicate, but Jennifer needed a little extra time to be exposed to sign language before she started to join in on the fun.

Just as she was not nimble enough to sign as an infant, however, I noticed how some signs were difficult for Jennifer's small hands to make. When this happened, we created home signs to use instead. *Home signs* are signs made up in place of an American Sign Language (ASL) sign for something. They're mostly used for babies who don't yet have enough manual dexterity to sign everything, but a lot of deaf families use them, too. One deaf mother shared with me her angst over the idea of not being able to communicate with her child if they didn't know the sign for something. In this way, home signs proved useful. In some cultures, home signs are used when there is not a word in that particular language for something. So for Jennifer, I allowed home signs until she was able to finally manage to make the correct sign for something. If anything, the two of us had fun making up signs for something we didn't know the real sign for. In some way, our special sign for something became a secret we enjoyed sharing.

A lot of books, videotapes, software and Internet articles are out there on how to teach a baby sign language, and it helps to ask other parents how they managed to do this. I've talked with so many deaf parents about this and can only cringe when I read about a *hearing* parent teaching her *hearing* child how to sign. I had to read many articles and browsed many books on how to do this, yet there was not one sure thing to do successfully to teach my baby how to sign. What worked for one child didn't work for the other.

Thankfully, a channel on TV has a segment where the host teaches young viewers a sign or two. Jesse is the one who watches that channel, and we've noticed how he'll often imitate the signs he sees on the screen. Jennifer and I have grabbed these moments and we all sit together making the signs we see the host and children making. When a television commercial airs where the person is singing a song while also signing some of the words, this, too, becomes an educational experience for all three of us. Even if Jennifer knows the signs, she'll still participate because it keeps her younger brother interested in participating, too.

One lesson I've learned in my attempts to teach my children sign language during their infant and toddler years is that patience is a *must.* I became too impatient with my first child in the beginning and I know this is what held up her learning how to sign. But I have to make sure I am patient with making sign language a part of our home life and keep at it over and over, day after day. Sometimes my children can't remember a sign very well, despite spending a good portion of one day using it, and that's okay. Sometimes, we forget things. The sign is again taught and there's that chuckle as she mutters, "Oh, right!"

Another lesson I learned from this is that I have to remember that teaching and learning sign language is a process. It won't be a smashing success overnight, but once it's learned and used as often as possible, sign language becomes not just an alternative way to communicate with others, but a primary language between a deaf parent and the hearing child.

Volume Control

Take one look at my TV set at any time while it's on and it will tell you one thing: Deaf *and* hearing people live here. The volume is on and there are captions at the bottom of the screen.

It wasn't always this way.

Before my husband and I had a child, we kept our TV volume muted because we had no way of knowing if it was too loud and bothering the neighbors. So, we didn't take that chance. After Jennifer took an interest in watching TV shows like *Blue's Clues* and *Little Bear*, and Jesse just couldn't go a day without enjoying *Caillou* or seeing Elmo on the screen, that's when the volume on the TV had to be turned back up.

The only problem was trying to figure out just how high that volume could go without being too loud.

Normally, what we did to test the volume of the TV was place our hand on the speaker. If it felt too loud, we'd turn it down. The problem with that method, though, was that it wasn't exactly perfect. One of my sisters visiting with us informed me of how the TV volume was too low, which I had previously thought was just right after feeling the speakers. So much for that idea!

I decided on a few other things to try to help fix the *volume control* problem.

Method 1: Use the number setting on the TV to determine the proper volume, asking a hearing person to listen until it's just right. Afterward, set the volume at this number.

Result: Not every TV shows a number for every time you hit the button to increase the volume. My TV doesn't have this, so that wasn't something I could try.

Method 2: Ask a hearing person to set the volume and leave it there.

Result: I actually tried this once. Silly me, thinking it would work. I was soon reminded of just how push-happy little ones can be with those buttons on a TV set. If they're not pounding away at the remote, they're at the TV changing channels, turning the volume up and down, and making pictures have a sudden snowstorm hit during what had been a summer vacation. Yes, my children soon became acquainted with all the fun things that happened whenever they pushed one of those buttons on the TV set. And once Jesse connected the remote control with doing nifty things on the TV set, he, too, started to interrupt our regularly scheduled program. I still chuckle over the time Jennifer used the remote to somehow or another order Pay-Per-View, yet I knew that letting something like that get out of hand meant a thinning wallet. At one point, I seriously started debating removing the button for the volume after feeling one too many earthquakes in the living room just because the volume on the TV set was too high.

Method 3: Ask child or a hearing person to say when the volume is just right then turn it all the way down, counting each and every tap of the minus key on the remote, then counting as you increase it back to the number you counted to.

Result: *This* is the tried and true method that has worked best for us. This is *the* number one thing we have learned to do when it comes to adjusting the volume on the TV. Sometimes it's not perfect. Some movies and TV shows have different volume levels (a fact of life that shall forever remain a mystery to me), so sometimes it needs to go up just a little bit more or down just a little bit more.

But when it comes to setting the TV at normal volume, we use this other numbering system. We just count how many pushes on the button it takes to get there.

Sometimes our little ones like to take over the remote control. No matter where we hide it or how far we put it up, they always manage to get to it. Sometimes *Jennifer* wants to be the one to decide if the TV is loud enough. Or low enough.

Most of the time, though, I trust Jennifer's judgment. She'll usually let us know if the TV set is too loud. If we get to the point where she can't hear us telling her something because the TV is too loud, however, we step in and turn it down. Also, because of our baby's sensitive eardrums, we adjust the volume once he starts covering his ears. (On the other hand, he has been known to turn the volume down if something is on the TV that he doesn't want to watch.)

All the same, we don't allow our kids to watch TV all day. During the time they *are* allowed to watch TV, and the occasional movie, we set the volume to where it is comfortable for all of us to enjoy.

When it came to volume on the radio, this one was a no-brainer. Thanks to our experiences in managing the volume on a TV set, I thought the easiest way to manage the volume on a radio is just to ask someone who can hear to listen and decide when the volume is set at a *safe* level of listening. This can be marked on the volume setting of the radio with a small piece of white tape. Then it could be marked with another strip of tape, possibly duct tape, where the volume is too loud.

As a deaf person living in a neighborhood that is predominantly hearing, I know I have to be mindful of the noise level coming out of my house. I don't mind noise from my neighbors, though my children have complained they couldn't sleep because of noise from the neighbors. All the same, we need to be respectful of just how loud, or quiet, things are in the home, since it's the hearing children enjoying those noisy things which the deaf parents need to keep watch over.

A Blessing in Disguise

Sometimes, too much research can be a bad thing. This is a lesson I learned one evening, as I did research for an article I was under deadline for. Somehow or another, I came across a BBC News article about a deaf lesbian couple who managed to ensure the baby they wanted would likewise be deaf. Employing the assistance of a sperm donor who came from a family with five generations of deafness, they got their wish—and ended up being publicly ostracized for their decision.

While I don't see how they did anything wrong—since, after all, they relied on a donor and not genetic screening—the whole issue reflected more on deaf couples wanting *deaf like me* babies.

In other words, deaf designer babies.

I kept clicking and clicking on links exploring this issue further. Eventually, my research took me to an article explaining the process of preimplantation genetic diagnosis, or PGD. By using embryo screening, the process of in-vitro fertilization (IVF) is used and the eggs and sperm are combined in a lab dish. Before the typical procedure that follows in which a viable embryo is implanted in the womb, PGD begins after three days. The embryos are screened to detect for certain diseases or disabilities. Up until recently, the process was used to weed out any embryos which harbored a child that would develop Down's syndrome or some other genetic disease. The healthy embryos were used for implantation and the *imperfect* ones were destroyed. However, PGD has been used to detect embryos that have the parents' desired gender, eye color and even if there is a potential for deafness.

All of this sparked what is known as *deaf designer babies.* Apparently, many deaf couples wanted babies who are born deaf just so they could share the same lifestyle or culture.

My research made me sickened when I read of one deaf couple who aborted their baby once they learned the child wasn't deaf, and further disgusted when someone commenting on one of the articles I read cited deafness as a *birth defect.*

But what angered me the most was how many of the readers responding to the articles I read always said *deaf couples* or *deaf parents* without putting *some* or *many* before that word pairing. Basically, one deaf couple's choice seemed to reflect the choice of *all* deaf couples in the world. Granted, many articles including deaf couples who preferred deaf babies noted they are in a small minority in the deaf community, yet many of the hearing readers commenting seemed to be under the impression that this is something *all* deaf couples want. As though we all want only deaf babies and will do what it takes to make sure we get them. It didn't help that one deaf mother was commenting on how she wished her hearing children had been born deaf, and, further, that she asked their doctor how to *fix* their hearing into deafness.

Reading all of these articles and comments made me stop and think. As a deaf parent with hearing children, I could not wrap my brain around why it is so terrible to be a deaf parent with hearing children. The thing I didn't hope for when I was pregnant with my children is not deafness, but instead simply a healthy baby. Is that really too much to ask?

Even so, looking further into this issue does help one to understand it better. These deaf parents want deaf children in order to promote and continue Deaf Culture in their home. As many may point out, you can't understand what it is like to be deaf unless you *are* deaf. In some way, perhaps it makes sense. But wouldn't it make even more sense to welcome a hearing child into the world? A hearing person who will grow to appreciate and respect the deaf community after witnessing it personally?

How would this whole thing of a deaf parent wanting a deaf designer baby justify telling your own child, "We didn't want you unless you were deaf?" Why should a parent's love be so conditional?

The next thing that turned up in my research on this topic was the lesbian couple's comment: "A hearing baby would be a blessing. A deaf baby would be a special blessing."

I'm sorry, did I miss something? I thought having a baby was enough of a blessing. I know women struggling with infertility would give *anything* to have a baby at all, and consider that baby a blessing whether the baby could hear or not hear, see or not see. I really don't see how there could be much difference between a child being a *blessing* and a *special blessing.*

I look at my experiences with my children and I could not imagine life being any other way. As a deaf parent with a hearing child, I can only say that I have no regrets and I would never trade my child for any other deaf child out there in the world. God has blessed me with these beautiful gifts which I have cherished. Because I have hearing children instead of deaf children, I do not feel unhappy, unfulfilled or under the impression that I have done the deaf world a great injustice. Maybe they will even appreciate it that, one day, there will be two hearing adults out there in the world who were raised by deaf parents, and as a result, know sign language, understand Deaf Culture and are sensitive to the issues affecting the deaf.

The feelings of sickness over reading about *deaf designer babies* and wanting only deaf babies faded after I read comments from other deaf parents who echoed my feelings. Many other deaf parents out there feel the same way I do: They are happy to even have a baby, whether that baby can hear or not. As one deaf parent commented, "I was hoping to have deaf children, but ended up having hearing children. They have been a blessing and I really enjoy having them. They also have opened my eyes to many things." There was also the following comment: "To wish for a deaf child who must struggle harder against the odds to achieve successfully in a hearing world is selfish. You expect the tax payers [sic] to foot the bill for your deaf child's expensive special education and interpreters? The financial responsibility should be 100% yours because you want a designer deaf baby!"

Being a deaf parent with a hearing child does change things, and those changes can be good changes. It means a long, hard road ahead, but that doesn't make me have second thoughts about having my hearing babies. I accept whatever lies ahead of me, whether my babies are hearing or deaf. I am content to be blessed with *any* kind of baby at all!

And, yes, giving birth to a happy, healthy baby *is,* in my opinion, a blessing. A special blessing in its own right. Who we are and what we do defines us, not what abilities or disabilities we may have.

I love my hearing children with my whole heart. I would still love them just the same if they were deaf. I love their personalities and their sweet looks. I marvel over my daughter's knack for figuring out puzzles and imitating TV characters, and my son's kooky way of dancing to music. I get a chuckle over watching my children imitate the way I talk and live, especially when I see them doing something which can only come from their father's genes.

The very thought of even taking their life away from them only because they can hear makes me feel a deep, painful sadness and a strong sickness. I think about all of the moments I would have missed out on: The beautiful moment of holding these babies in my arms right after they were born. The faces they made as newborns. The look of innocent surprise they make over sounds. The security and gratitude in knowing they can hear things that I can't. The opportunity to explore and be inspired by their hearing world, just as they are likewise inspired by my deaf world. And the profound gratitude which fills me over the fact that, no matter what happens, they will be able to witness first-hand just how human, resilient and adaptable a deaf person can be.

No matter what other people may think or feel, I still consider my hearing children to be a blessing. In fact, they are a *special blessing.* A blessing in disguise.

Fuzzy Lipreading

"How do you know she has a lisp?"

The question came during a chat I was having with a friend. I mentioned my daughter has a lisp and my friend, who has known me since high school, is well aware of just how profound my deafness is. My mentioning the lisp seemed to catch him by surprise.

"From lipreading her," I answered. But, actually, that's not how I learned Jennifer had a lisp.

It actually took some effort to even *lipread* her when she lisped.

I first got the heads-up one day when we were sitting at the computer, talking. We discussed an upcoming visit to my parents' house, and also of seeing my younger brother and his four children there. "We'll get to see Little Guy, Noah and J.J.!" I gushed.

"And we'll get to see BLANK," Jennifer said.

I studied her. "Who?" What she said didn't *look* like a familiar name. I knew it was a "W" word but couldn't understand what came after it.

She again said the name but I still didn't understand her. Finally, she pointed at the computer monitor, which has the screensaver showing pictures of family. She pointed at the picture of my niece, Laurie, and said, "Waurie."

At first, I didn't think I got that right. I asked her, "Did you say *Waurie?*"

She nodded.

I asked her again. "Did you say *Waurie?* Your cousin, Laurie?"

She nodded again, though this time, she seemed confused, as if she'd done something wrong.

Well, she *had,* but not in the way she thought she had.

I was still uncertain, though. I just didn't think I'd understood her correctly. And maybe she hadn't understood me correctly, either. Maybe she had just said the name that way on a lark. Maybe she wouldn't *normally* say the name that way.

One of my sisters, who can hear, later solved this mystery. I had Jennifer say the name *Laurie* in front of her and she confirmed that my daughter had indeed said the name as *Waurie.*

As it turned out, Jennifer said other *L* words with a *W,* as well. I noticed how she'd say, "I wove you, Mommy." When I made her food a certain way, she'd perk up and say, "I wike it!" And as I watched her say her bedtime prayers one evening, I almost chuckled when she said, "I pray my Ward [Lord] my soul to keep."

She also had a problem saying words with *TH* in them. She'd say *teef* instead of *teeth.* Or *wiff* instead of *with.* There was also *brover* instead of *brother.*

As cute as this was, I felt concern. I mean, Jennifer *is* my first child, and I can't remember much from my childhood of anybody lisping in the family that resulted in permanent speech difficulties. My younger brother did have a speech problem when he was a kid, but he eventually grew out of it. I worried this might be a speech problem or that she'd still be saying *I wike it!* while in her 30s.

I didn't know what to do, so I chatted with a family member, Allison, about it. The first thing Allison said was that this was not a lisp, but a speech impediment. Allison assured me Jennifer would eventually grow out of it and not to worry. After Jennifer started school, they would help her to say her words better, she assured. She also reminded me of another niece who used to do the same thing, and how speech specialists at her school worked with her to correct the problem.

That helped me to feel more at ease and I decided I'd just wait it out. Wait a while or wait until she started kindergarten before I let it be a concern again. Just relish this *baby talk* my baby was using and rest assured it wasn't going to result in imperfect speech or slow speech development later on.

Time passed, and it wasn't long before I didn't want to keep waiting anymore. In fact, the longer this continued, as one year passed and the next with this lisping still going on, the more worried and frustrated I grew.

Eventually, I decided to take matters into my own hands. Try to correct her lisping myself. Granted, I'm no speech specialist or some kind of language development expert, but it started to really bug me how Jennifer called her friend Lilly, *Willy,* and said she was *ready for bidness* after I commented she looked *ready for business.*

I started to work with her in saying her words correctly. I would get on my knees, face to face with her, then *very slowly* and with exaggerated mouth movements, I would say the words the right way.

"*LLLaurie.* Not Waurie."

"*Pillllow.* Not piwwow."

"*LLLord.* Not Ward."

"*Bu-si-ness.* Not bidness."

"*Tee-th.* Not teef."

"*LLLike.* Not wike."

She would eventually say the words correctly after a couple of tries in repeating me, but it soon happened that she went right back to saying *Waurie, piwwow, Ward, bidness, teef* and *wike.*

At one point, flabbergasted over the whole thing, I just threw up my arms and asked her, "Jennifer, why do you say the words like that?"

She would only look at me, confused. I might as well have just asked her how to perform brain surgery. Finally, she'd shrug her shoulders and say, "I don't know."

After some more time passed and my efforts to correct this lisp failed miserably, I just grew to accept it. After all, she *was* still my baby and not even in school yet. *Perhaps,* I thought, *the schools would do a better job at correcting the lisp.* Perhaps she *would* grow out of it. For the time being, I cherished this *baby talk,* because something told me it wouldn't be long before she wasn't a baby anymore. As one parent on a message board commented about this, "For goodness sake, be patient. Once she has learned, you will miss her *widdle teef* talking to the *Ward."*

This person was right. Jennifer was six years old at the time the worry was really kicking in. I discussed it with her teacher, and a speech therapist was enlisted to work with her, just as I did.

By the time she was eight, Jennifer did grow out of saying words that way, and I'm relieved she doesn't say things like *I need to brush my teef* anymore.

I had to remind myself, *this, too, shall pass* after Jesse started talking the same way, when he was a preschooler. His pediatrician couldn't help but notice this, but all he asked was if his preschool teacher understood him. Going through this the second time, there is less worry and anxiety. Researching this on the Internet, I was further calmed by the fact that there are so many other parents out there whose toddlers and preschoolers do the same thing. Some parents assured others the child would grow out of this, and, if not, then a speech therapist at the school would assist. One big message I saw in my research was how important it was to correct this early, because if it was not corrected, then it would cause other speech problems later on.

We as a family chuckle about these speech goofs for now and are more relaxed knowing that this is not something which will permanently affect Jesse's speech. If he doesn't outgrow it then, eventually, there are speech therapists at the school who can help him along just as they helped Jennifer. Until then, Jesse says *fank you* when something is done for him and we all *wove* each other all the same.

The Identity Crisis

A small hand was patting my leg. "Dawn! Dawn! Dawn!" a voice cried out with excitement.

I looked to see who it was saying my name and my eyes fell on . . . my toddler. Instead of calling me *Mom,* she called me by my name. This wasn't the first time it's happened, and every time it occurred, I couldn't help but wonder when that would change. How long before she stopped calling me by name and refereed to me with that magical word I loved seeing come from her lips: *Mom.*

Every mother loves to hear their child call them, *Mama.* Or *Mom,* or *Mommy.* This is our affirmation that we are this little angel's mommy: protector, caregiver, cheerleader, and teacher. Until sign language was learned, I relied on lipreading to understand what Jennifer said when she said *Mom.* But at this time in her life, she was not saying it yet.

As a toddler, Jennifer hardly called me Mama. Or even Mom or Mommy. Any time she wanted to get my attention, she had patted my leg, crying out, "Dawn! Dawn! Dawn!"

This happened regardless of how fast I gave her my attention; she always called my name out three times. Of course, I laughed myself silly over these moments. She acted with such urgency whether she wanted to show me that she found a clue in one of her *Blue's Clues* books or that there was a bird up in the sky.

Still, I wondered why she called me by my name. My husband hardly said my name around her, and my parents no longer lived by us, meaning she didn't hear them referring to me by name every day. On the other hand, calling me Mam" happened when she wanted to get out of her crib, and Dawn was used for all the other times.

Two of my sisters went through the same thing: Their children called them by their names instead of calling them Mom. My older sister even had her son refer to her by a shortened version of her name.

During those early years of her life, I knew Jennifer understood I'm her mommy, even when she didn't call me that. It would have been nice if she called me Mama more often, but what mattered is that, at least, she knew who she wanted when she called out my name.

Later, as she got older, she started calling me Mom as well as Mommy. She also called me Mama and even the irritating, "Moo-oo-oom," during her whining episodes.

After her little brother entered the picture, he always called me Mama, Mom or Mommy, but there were a couple of times he did refer to me by name. Nevertheless, he calls me Mom most of the time.

It's not a huge issue, though. I know who they are calling for, and so do they.

PART FOUR:

Making Deaf Parenting Work

Baby-proofing the Home, the Deaf Parent's Way

You've seen them: Books and articles blaring titles that promise a safer home for your baby. "Error-proof your kitchen." *Baby-Proofing Basics.* "Baby-proof an Apartment." *Child Safe: A Practical Guide for Preventing Childhood Injuries.* I read anything and everything I could get my hands on before my child was born. Sure I'd grown up in a home with small children, and I've stayed in homes with babies, but pregnancy seemed to have an additional side effect: Amnesia. It's like all of a sudden, everything I knew about caring for a baby and baby-proofing my home became subjects unknown to me. For this reason, I dove into reading everything I could find, even through the Internet.

The one thing I wanted to cover all the bases on was baby-proofing my home. Unfortunately, there wasn't a whole lot of material out there on how a *deaf* parent should baby-proof their home. In fact, I found very little information available.

This may not seem like such a big issue but, being a deaf parent, a few tips on baby-proofing strategies really would have come in handy.

Having the home baby-proofed as much as possible is a really big help. A baby-proofed home really set my mind at ease, knowing that my crawling/walking children wouldn't get hurt so easily in their own home. This doesn't mean I could take a break on keeping a constant watch on them—I still got up to check on them every few minutes while they played in another room—but it just makes life a little easier, more for myself than for my babies.

And because I can't hear, certain changes had to be made in my child's home environment. The living environment of a disabled person is different from that of a non-disabled person, and this is also true when it comes to being a parent. There are different accouterments in the home and different rules to follow.

The Baby Cryer, a device which alerts a sleeping parent to the baby's cries by vibrating their mattress, is first and foremost one important tool in a deaf parent's home. I have seen some monitors with portable screens on them, allowing the parent to see the baby. I have never used them, but it wouldn't hurt in using it as a baby-proofing tool.

Besides using the Baby Cryer, I also found it was a good idea to have locks on the doors. My husband put inexpensive hook locks on all the doors and a latch lock on the door to the water heater after our child started opening doors. This really helped us keep an eye on where she was going. We even have a lock on the door to the linen closet because, even though Jennifer was able to get inside of the closet, she had a hard time getting out of it. I made this discovery one day when I found her in there, crying because she'd been unable to get out. A lock on that door prevented a repeat of that situation.

If our children want in our bedroom, they'd have to ask one of us to unlock the door first. This way, not only were we alerted to them being in a room they're not usually allowed inside, but it also prompted an adult to be in there with them to ensure they didn't get into something they shouldn't.

This brings me to another point. We had to keep *everything* the baby can't have up high (like in a high kitchen cabinet) or behind a locked door. We keep scissors, markers, lighters, medicine, board games, important/expensive books, light bulbs and other dangerous items out of the children's reach. After one too many occasions of Jennifer drawing on the walls or Jesse coloring on his legs, we had to put all crayons, markers and ink pens into a plastic tote, high up on a shelf in the closet. If the kids wanted to color or needed a pencil, they had to ask us for help to get them, and that way we could monitor them while they did whatever they wanted to do.

Keeping everything out of the baby's reach is a good idea even for something we don't *think* our child can break or hurt herself with. If parenting has taught me anything, it's the power of Murphy's Law. One day I had a lamp with a broken lampshade sitting on the center of the kitchen table, waiting to be fixed. Jennifer climbed up on the chairs, grabbed the cord (which of course

I had wrapped around the lamp), untangled it, wrapped it around the backs of the chairs circling the table, then *pulled.* I didn't discover the broken lamp until after she'd happily trotted off to her room. (My consolation was that it was an ugly lamp, anyway.)

Likewise, I just don't take the chance that something is put away high enough or in a safe place. A cup of coffee I had on the mantel one day was almost attacked by my toddler son's hands, and my rushing over to the scene prevented him from getting burned by the hot liquid. For this reason, I keep in mind that, somehow or another, the baby *could* get to something or *could* open something. So even with locks and caution, and putting things up high, I still have to keep watch to make sure the children don't get hurt.

Another thing I had to learn as far as baby-proofing a deaf parent's home is that it's a good idea to keep all appliances the baby can reach unplugged. Actually, it's a *very* good idea. One day, I was sitting at the computer, checking my email, when I started to smell a funny odor. I ran to the kitchen only to discover that Jennifer had put a coaster into the microwave then turned it on! I learned two things that day:

#1) The microwave, toaster, coffee maker and crock pot all must remain unplugged when not in use. (I keep them on my countertops but, as every parent of a toddler knows, small children have a knack for climbing onto the kitchen counters! They also seem to have a knack for figuring out how to turn everything on.) And

#2) Coasters don't smell very good when they melt.

Of course, some appliances may have to stay plugged in while in use, and even then, keep them *away* from the edge of the counter. We once had a coffeemaker that allowed people to press their cup against a latch to fill with coffee. You would think this is convenient for parents trying to get a cup of coffee while holding a baby in their arms, right? But it's not so good for a child who is tall enough to reach the latch. One thing that can happen if such an item is too close to the counter's edge is that a child can easily reach up to the latch and scald their hands when they release the hot liquid. But the other thing that can happen is what happened to Jennifer when she backed up against the counter where the coffeemaker was. Her shoulder rested against the latch and hot coffee came down, burning her shoulder. We moved that coffeemaker away from the counter's edge, but eventually decided to go back to using a regular coffeemaker instead.

One other thing that's come in handy is the baby gate. Sure, all parents use them to block staircases and such, but, being a deaf parent, I discovered the value of having a baby gate in a whole new way. For me, the baby gate came in handy during the times I was in the kitchen cooking a meal. My small kitchen gave me the luxury of barricading the area between the sink and stove, areas I couldn't have my children in while I was busy cooking dinner. I wouldn't be able to hear them scream if they put their hand on the burner while I'm at the sink, my back turned from them, draining a pan. It's also helpful because I move around so much between the cabinets, sink and stove when I cook, and bumping into one of them when they're right behind me means I might spill something hot on them. As the kids grew older, though, I could not continue using a baby gate to barricade the kitchen, so it became a habit to look behind me first to make sure the coast was clear before moving away from the stove carrying a hot pan of food. I did try telling the children to stay out of the kitchen when I was cooking, but this was not always possible, especially when the kids played and ran around the house when I was cooking something. Even so, always look first to make sure little ones are not underfoot.

When Jennifer was a toddler, I set up the baby gate to cordon off the kitchen. For the most part, my daughter would sit on the floor in front of a cabinet I kept filled with plastic bowls and cups for her to play with while I cooked. Sometimes, she'd empty the cabinet then crawl inside and fall asleep in there. There were times she'd also sit at the kitchen table coloring, all where I could see her as I cooked. Of course, there were times I had to go check on her if she was in another room as I cooked, but having that baby gate there to keep her from wandering up to the stove and burning herself really gave me a huge peace of mind. With Jesse, I'd set him up in the highchair in the kitchen and give him a few toys to play with. He seemed to enjoy this situation, often watching Mommy with a curious stare as I cooked dinner, and rubbing his tummy over the smells of the yummy food cooking on the stove.

The baby gate is great for blocking hallways when everyone is asleep at night, too. This prevented Jennifer from getting up in the middle of the night and wandering around the house without being able to alert her sleeping parents should any noises happen. (With Jesse, however, that is another story which I share later on in this book.) Still, it did still have its uses.

In the event that a baby gate couldn't be used in the kitchen, though, I had to be extra careful when I had a stove turned on. I had to keep as close an eye on my children as possible and remember to look behind myself *first* before turning around.

Safety must begin at home, and every deaf parent wants their child to be in a safe environment. It's up to us to use whatever tools we can to ensure our children are in a safe home and using extra care when those tools are not available.

Baby-proofing my home doesn't guarantee my child can freely roam about without supervision, but it *does* provide me with a sound peace of mind. At least I know my child is in a safe home, and that effort to ensure her safety is only half the battle.

Family Support: The Lifeline for All Parents

The baby was crying. Not just crying. *Really* crying. Like something was very wrong crying.

Maybe it was her diaper? No; diaper was clean and dry.

Maybe she was hot. After adjusting her clothes, she still screamed and cried.

I struggled to understand what was wrong. *Is she uncomfortable?* Moving her to another location, carrying her around and rocking her did nothing to soothe her cries.

She didn't look good. Maybe she was in pain. Why would she be in pain? There were no obvious injuries. She hadn't been in anything. Her clothes were loose and not restricting at all.

I thought of other things. Colic. Could it be colic? How could it be colic? It's daytime. She's never been colicky before.

Call Mom. That's the advice from my instincts. Call Mom and ask her what could be wrong.

No. Wait. Can't call Mom. Can't do that. Must be able to handle this parenting stuff all on my own. Deaf capable parent here! Everything is fine and under control.

Then Reason grabbed me by the collar and screamed, "The baby is crying! You need to *do* something!"

I watched my hand move as I turned on the TTY and my fingers started hitting the keys. The plea for help was made: "Mom, the baby is crying. I've checked everything. What could be the problem?"

I held my breath. Here comes the accusation, I thought. I am a bad parent. I can't take care of my own baby without help. I can't do this parenting thing!

I prepared for a verbal onslaught. I braced myself for the harsh words, the criticism, the attack on me as a deaf person and as a deaf parent.

But the attack never came. The very first words out of my mother's mouth were not judgmental, but helpful: "Well, maybe she is teething."

Teething! Yes! Of course! That's it! She's *teething*!

The baby was given teething gel on her gums and a teething ring to suck on.

And . . . she stopped crying. Just like that. Peace was restored in our home. The clouds opened and sunlight shone in.

Relief flooded through me as I held my peaceful baby in my arms. Relief that a solution had been found. Relief that my mother didn't say one word of accusation to me at all the very first time I reached out to her for help. She only offered support, not judgment. There I was, ready for her to accuse me of being a bad deaf mother because I didn't know what to do to help my crying baby. But all along, she was ready to offer her support instead.

And because she offered her support so freely, so quickly, my little baby's pain was brought to an end. There was nothing prolonging her misery. No grandmother bickering with her mother about how it was a bad idea to become a parent because she is deaf. Just like that, the decision to instead be supportive was made. Just like that, we worked together to help a baby who was in pain.

When I realized that it was perfectly okay to go to my mother for help whenever some parenting emergency came up, a sense of gratitude overcame me. I was grateful to her for not judging me and for being supportive. This told me she was not going to criticize my lack of abilities as a new parent. It also told me that anytime I needed her, for anything, she was there. She didn't see me as a deaf person with a new baby to care for; she saw me as a brand new parent who needed her wisdom and expertise to get through this new chapter in life. Her door was always open anytime I needed her, and I *did* need her.

During my first pregnancy, I practically had my obstetrician's number on speed dial. I constantly called his office, asking about every little thing. Even on the day I gave birth, I was still asking questions. In fact, one nurse gave me a knowing look and asked, "This is your first baby, isn't it?"

Then the baby was born. Then I finally understood it was perfectly fine to call my mother for help about any old thing and to ask any questions I had. And as a new parent, I had a lot. Thankfully, my mother was there to answer them all, and she answered many more after the second baby was born and we went through new experiences.

Before Jennifer was born, I'd longed for a child. In fact, it took me more than two years to conceive her! My desire to become a parent burned within me, transcending all fears, anxieties and challenges I would face because I am deaf.

Having my mother stand behind me and support that desire to become a parent was an advantage which I was sad to learn many other deaf parents did not have. I've read of siblings stepping in *for the sake of the child* and taking over the parenting duties the deaf parent is responsible for, all because they feel the deaf parent cannot live up to those responsibilities. Or perhaps they think you need to hear to be a good parent, since the ability to listen for a crying baby is not there. These families are trapped by their old-fashioned ideas that you need to have *all* of your abilities with you in order to be a good parent. You need to hear, you need to see, you need to be able to walk, talk and think. Never mind that humans can adapt, and that brand new parents with disabilities are often willing to adapt to their limited environments. The biggest price that is paid, however, is the bond that should be there between parent and child. The connection between a child with their deaf mother or father is lost, and this is often left out of the equation when hearing family members step in to take over in the child's life. It's like tearing the child away from the heart of their mother or father, who means the world to them in this huge, scary world they have been brought into.

These actions, which appear to be *good intentions* to the hearing family members, can actually be detrimental to the child's perceptions of his or her parents. Because someone else is taking over the parental duties, the child perceives that their mother or father has *failed* them as a mother or father. Additionally, this also tells the child that because someone is deaf, they cannot be good parents. The hearing family member discriminating against a deaf person trying to be a good parent is only teaching the child discrimination against the deaf.

The irony is that, as a parent or a sibling, these hearing family members should by now understand this deaf person's abilities. As family, there should be encouragement and the desire to push this deaf person to be a better person. Instead of fighting with each other, they should by now understand this deaf person's abilities to do what needs to be done in this new role as a parent and be there to offer support when that support is needed. If those abilities are not there, they should work together to make everything right for the child. Causing drama, passing judgments and being critical of the new deaf parent does nothing to improve the situation. This deaf person is a brand new parent, after all. Babies do not come with instructions. The new parent does have the advantage of an experienced and wizened parent in the family to offer support and guidance when that is needed—the same goes even if that parent is disabled. Chances are good that guidance and advice will often be needed.

They say that it takes a village to raise a child. What needs to be a part of that *village* is support for the brand new parent who may not be as experienced as the others may be. We turn to people with experience to help us navigate these strange waters. It's a natural instinct to find an *expert* when we can't figure things out on our own. Some of the people we seek out for help should, ideally, be family members. Parents, siblings, relatives.

Our family is where we come from, where we draw our strength from and where we learn how to survive this adventure called *life.* We derive our beliefs and our heritage from our family, continuing the generations with the advice, wisdom and stories passed down to us from our predecessors. The world itself can be a cruel and unforgiving place, and having our family to turn to and find comfort from helps us to be stronger and more resilient. Even so, having that family there to turn to in a world that discriminates against the deaf and hard-of-hearing can make this scary experience of being a new parent not so scary anymore. It helps us to be a better person and a better deaf parent, because the support from the family makes this journey all the more meaningful.

Knowing that our family is behind us as we grow and learn as a parent will help us feel more confident and secure to get through the challenging times every parenting experience is bound to include. When that support from our family is not there, we stumble. We fall.

When it comes to whether or not a family will support the brand new parent, deafness should not be the issue. Disability should not be the issue. Unfortunately, many families have made this an issue. They want the drama. They want the old-fashioned ideas. They want the wall they build between themselves and their deaf offspring to stay right where it is, thank you very much.

When that happens, negative messages are sent from these hearing family members. Despite the inability to hear audibly, the deaf parent will hear this subliminal message loud and clear: "I can't support your new role as a parent because you are deaf. I won't stand behind you or respect your wishes to be a parent because you are deaf.

If you want support, go find support from somebody else. Don't come to me."

Granted, it's not realistic to expect every family out there in the world to be supportive of a deaf parent. I know there will be entire families against a deaf person's wishes to be a parent, and even certain family members. I know this too well. I come from a family where drama is our religion. Some family members have been supportive, some have not. That's a given for every family, whether or not someone is deaf or blind or with limited mobility.

But if there is *one person* who will offer that much-needed support—just one—then that's all the deaf parent needs. That one source of support is enough. And that one source of support will make a difference.

Experience has taught me to find that support and advice from a family member who is also a parent, because a lot of people who are not parents think they know *everything* there is to know about parenting, thanks to books they have read or something they saw on *Dr. Phil.* If you want support from your family, try turning to a fellow parent. Maybe this is why my mother was so eager to offer support because, once upon a time, she had been in my shoes.

Fortunately, there is more than one person in my family who offered support as I learned, and continue to learn, as a parent, not just as a deaf parent. My mother is one of those people, and she joins the others who I know I can turn to if another situation comes up where I just don't know what to do. They are the gentle touch, the guiding hand and the soft voice of encouragement. They are my center. My one source of strength.

Should another emergency come up, it is comforting to know just where I can go and who I can turn to for help. Because of them, the journey as a deaf parent is not so uncertain. It is accompanied by experienced parents ready to guide this tiny bundle of life into adulthood. I may not have all the answers as a parent and may not always know what to do, but because of family support, there is someone who will always be there to help out and bring peace.

Joining the Ranks: Networking with Other Deaf Parents

Sometimes I saw them at a monthly social, but at all times I have found them online. It's not really too difficult never to see one when I'm running errands, and some who I have never met before send me an email.

These are the deaf parents I network with, the same people I share all of my parenting joys, woes, stories and concerns with. They are various ages, various races and have one or more children, but the one thing we have in common is the thing that draws us together: being a deaf parent. I have heard of CODAs (children of deaf adults) forming some kind of bond with each other through the simple fact that their parents are deaf, and in the same way I think a bond can likewise develop between deaf parents.

I have had the good fortune to experience this part of my life with so many different people, in real life and through the Internet. Almost all of the people who have been involved in my parenting experiences could hear and while they offered so much advice, support and assistance, I never had the same *kinship* which I developed from networking with other deaf parents. First and foremost, I am deaf, and I bring the same concerns, fears and issues of living in the deaf world to my world as a parent. Another deaf parent who feels the same fears and concerns would effectively be able to discuss them with me and not in the same way a hearing person would be able to. For example, a hearing person might address discrimination with the rhetorical question: "Isn't there a law against that?" Whereas a deaf person would relate to this personally and be able to offer a solution which they themselves might have used. I'm not trying to say a hearing parent's advice is useless to me; on the contrary, I've received very helpful information from hearing parents. But another deaf parent coping with the same worries of being able to sleep through the night without worrying over their child's safety could offer better advice because they've been there. There are just so many things we can talk about that a hearing parent wouldn't understand or relate to.

Of course I have been blessed in having helpful hearing parents at the ready to offer advice and assistance. My mom, some of my sisters and sisters-in-law were always ready to offer advice and swap parenting stories. Yet I have found, in talking with other deaf parents, the same helpful and engaging stories that I could apply from the experience of being deaf. I have been grateful for the opportunity to experience both sides of the coin, but I think a deaf parent would benefit enormously in having another deaf parent to share stories with. It just really helps. It makes me feel like I've got a support system on those days I can't lipread my child, or a business refuses to accept relay calls.

I happened upon a local deaf group by accident: I found them on Yahoo! I contacted the moderator and we *met* through email until, one day, we got together in person. She told me all about the group, signed me up to their mailing list, and it wasn't long before I had a group of local deaf parents just a mouse-click away to chat with. Up until then, I relied on Usenet to participate in an online group of deaf parents. The local group gives me the chance to meet them face-to-face, although this doesn't mean there's not much to gain in participating in an online-only group.

Another way I have networked with other deaf parents is when they email me. They'll find my email address in deaf message boards, through *SIGNews*, and when I have something deaf-related published somewhere. After my essay on being a deaf mother was published in *Mothering Magazine,* for example, deaf mothers emailed me to share their experiences. I have also met other deaf parents while writing articles on deaf parenting for *SIGNews*.

The Internet is a goldmine for finding like-minded and like-disabled people from other corners of the world. There are groups like those that can be found on Yahoo!, organizations for the deaf, through emailing other deaf parents I read about or see online, Twitter, visiting message boards for the deaf and checking out the chat rooms. The local YMCA/YWCA or a senior center with *deaf clubs* or *deaf support group* meetings is another option. A local college may offer information on any local deaf groups or events, and the National Association for the Deaf has a website (http://www.nad.org) listing deaf support groups. There is also the Hearing Loss Association of America (formerly SHHH, http://www.hearingloss.org/) and the Center on Deafness-Inland Empire (CODIE, http://codie .org/).

Another way to network with other deaf parents is through a community deaf/HOH event called *deaf coffee* or *silent coffee.* With these events, deaf and hard-of-hearing residents in a city meet with each other at a local coffeehouse and discuss issues or events. While deaf coffee groups are not in every single city of every single state, it's possible to find local deaf residents and see if you can arrange for a deaf coffee meeting in your area. For the record, you don't need to be a coffee drinker to attend. I've heard of groups meeting at pizzerias and bowling alleys. Again, use your search engine.

If using the Internet to find other deaf parents to network with isn't an option and there's nothing going on locally, there is always the option of starting a deaf parenting group or deaf support group where you live. Being able to do this really depends on how many deaf parents there are in the area. Placing an ad in the local paper to see if anyone's interested or putting out a flyer might also help. If anyone wants to get in on this, meetings can be arranged. Another option in lieu of getting together in person is to send out a bimonthly newsletter.

No journey should be traveled alone. I used to think that I didn't *need* other deaf parents to help me get through this experience; boy, was I wrong! There are so many times that sharing stories about being a deaf parent has helped me to get through it just a little bit stronger, if not clued me in on some tips and techniques. Knowing that another deaf parent is out there going through the same exact obstacles I face helps alleviate the stress and nurtures support. Together, we can both overcome these problems and be ready to offer these experiences to other deaf parents, too. Getting support and advice from other deaf parents and being there to offer that same support and advice to other deaf parents out there just makes the journey a little bit easier.

On the Blogroll: Networking with Other Deaf Parents through Blogs

When blogs became popular in the late 1990s, they also opened a new outlet for deaf parents to network. Thanks to blogs, we could all talk about the experiences and issues affecting us, and sharing these experiences with others. When I started blogging in early 2000, I didn't create a blog with a *deaf parent* angle. In fact, it never occurred to me that just such an angle could be there. It wasn't until I *met* with another deaf mom via the Internet that I became aware of how having a *deaf blog* could benefit other deaf parents.

Karen Putz first contacted me by email. A writer herself, Karen commented on one of my books she'd found on the Internet and from then on, we became fast friends, sharing our stories as deaf parents and *talking shop* as writers. Karen steered me to her blog, A Deaf Mom Shares Her World (http://deafmomworld.com/) and I soon became immersed in a world where everything deaf was covered. Karen blogged not only about her experiences as a deaf mom but on the articles she wrote for *Hands & Voices*, news items affecting Gallaudett University, and other deaf/hard-of-hearing people she met. (As a regional representative for *Hands & Voices*, she met a lot of them!)

Reading Karen's blog soon became an educational experience for me. It also enriched my life as a deaf parent. Reading about experiences I went through, too, I no longer felt so alone or lost without someone to talk to about things. Whenever I got angry over being discriminated against because of my deafness or if something troubled me because I just didn't know how to handle it, Karen always had something to say about it in her blog, and her posts always seemed to be straight on the mark. As a deaf parent herself, she could understand what I was going through. Best of all, other deaf parents she knew would leave comments. Not only did this allow me the opportunity to read *their* blogs, but it also added more feedback on certain topics.

While I understand that I could still gain this experience from reading newspapers like *SIGNews* or magazines such as *Deaf Success*, the blogs maintained by deaf parents helped offer a more personal, direct glimpse into these experiences. The feedback left by others added to the diversity of these topics, but it also helped me to see them in a more broad, raw perspective. Not only this, but the blog posts covered a wide range of topics and experiences, things normally not covered so widely in the print media.

The networking wasn't limited to comments left on these blogs, however. I learned of a site called deafread.com, which included an exhaustive list of blogs maintained by other deaf/HOH people (and not just other deaf parents). Thanks to deafread.com, my reading experience of other deaf blogs became further enriched and more inspiring.

Although blogs are not generally considered to be a legit form of media the reading world can enjoy (not yet, anyway), they have still proven to be useful. For the blogs that don't just act as public *diaries* or albums of photos, the reading world can benefit immensely from the discussions and sharing of ideas inherent in many blogs today. This is especially true of the deaf world, where that feeling of isolation and being left out isn't so pervasive, thanks to blogs being majorly based on the ability to read and not hear. Deaf blogs are just one more form of specialized niche we find in the media, in the same category as audio books and magazines for the physically challenged. The only thing separating these blogs from the rest of the blogosphere and legitimate forms of media for the deaf world is their diverse coverage of real-world experiences. There's greater variety in what is covered, greater openness on what gets talked about, and no fears of discrimination or ignorance. There are no gatekeepers, no doubts over being politically correct (PC), and no limit to what can be blogged about. With blogs, anything can happen—and it usually does.

I don't keep a deaf-only blog, at my Palms to Pines blog (http://palmstopines.blogspot.com/), but because I have a blog which covers my personal life, and because I *am* deaf, there will be the occasional deaf-related blog post. One such blog post, titled "Talk and repeat," shortly ran after the blog got started in August 2006:

Often, when I'm talking with my neighbor, he'll ask me to repeat something I've said (unless our conversation is on a sheet of paper). I sometimes ask if there's too much noise either in his house or from traffic outside, but one of the reasons he'll ask me to repeat something is because I don't talk loud enough.

That's actually been a common problem of mine.

I once got into the habit of speaking "loudly," even though I didn't know if my voice was loud enough. And sometimes I'd have to ask people if they heard me or if I said something loud enough. Sometimes I'd repeat something I said because I'd think I didn't say it loud enough the first time, and I'd get a dirty look because people thought I was being moody or pushy. (I'd politely explain that I am deaf and I didn't know if I spoke loud enough the first time.) And then there were the many times when, if someone was with me, they'd discreetly let me know to speak louder and there was that understanding that I didn't know if I was speaking loud enough.

My mom once told me that after I lost my hearing, she would constantly encourage me to use my voice as much as possible. She had heard people who became deaf often stopped speaking since they mostly relied on ASL to communicate, anyway, and their voices sort of diminished because they didn't use them often enough. I rarely, if ever, stopped speaking, even when I was using ASL. Oh, sure, I would sometimes mutely sign to friends in high school, but mostly it didn't make sense to talk, anyway (like once when we communicated through the windows of a bus). But I didn't stop speaking even when I signed. After all, I'd lipread interpreters in high school, and it was because of the fact they spoke as they signed that I learned certain signs for words faster.

Admittedly, though, it can be difficult, lipreading someone AND looking at the signs at the same time. When I'm at church, that's pretty much what I do. My interpreter will speak as she signs to me. All the same, a lot of people who are deaf don't speak while they sign. I mean, if the person they are signing to understands them, they don't really need to speak. However, when a hearing person signs to me, he/she usually speaks as she signs. And I usually rely on the lipreading most of the time (that's pretty much relied on ever since I lost my hearing—that and written communication).

Still, I obviously have a hard time speaking loud enough. Just today, while my daughter rode the Big Wheel that belongs to my neighbor's daughter, I called out to her, "Did you have fun with Kristi today?" She came up to me and asked, "What did you say?"

Oy.

Yes, I live on a busy street. But there weren't any cars driving by. And I thought I had called out to her loud enough. Obviously, I hadn't.

Obviously, talking louder is something I still need to work on. Again.

My blog isn't exactly very popular (the above post received no comments), but it has been useful to me on a personal level in that at least I can get things off my chest and talk about how certain experiences, news items and issues (both deaf- and non-deaf-related) affect me in my own way. It's a great platform for me to share how I feel about things related to being a deaf parent. And it's a great way for us deaf parents to have open discussions on the things we wouldn't get to read or talk about in the print media.

Going it Alone: Lessons Learned as a Divorced Deaf Parent

After ten years together, my daughter's father and I finally married in the winter of 2002, when she was a year old. Unfortunately, that marriage didn't last for very long; I filed for divorce in the summer of 2006.

Our marriage had taken place in the California desert, where both of us had family living nearby. When we divorced, we were living in Eugene, Oregon, where I barely knew a soul. Had I lived closer to my family, I would've had their help and security as a newly single deaf parent. Instead, I was living somewhere with no friends, no relatives—and no idea of how to get through it all.

I wasn't, however, going to let my anxiety keep me from doing my job. I was *still* Jennifer's mother and I *still* had to own up to my new responsibilities each and every day. Now, I just had to do it alone.

Even as I struggled with my anxieties, I knew I couldn't allow them to cripple me. On the outside, I was a strong, confident Mommy. On the inside, I was scared to death.

Safety was my biggest concern. I mean, I couldn't hear *anything.* What if something happened to my child while I slept? What if someone tricked me into letting them in? What if I got hurt and Jennifer didn't know what to do?

A whole swarm of *what ifs* hovered over me, constantly weighing me down. To top all of that off, I was dealing with the guilt of breaking up our small family. Jennifer's dad only lived about ten minutes away, and even though she saw him every day and stayed with him on the weekends, she was still torn up over the fact that he didn't live with us anymore. True to form as a *Daddy's little girl,* she often watched for him at the living room window around the time he got off work. When she was not spending time with her father, she kept asking me why I wasn't married to him anymore.

These were divorce realities I hadn't been prepared to face, but I knew I had to do *something.* It was up to me now to take care of us, and I knew I had to take action.

—Set up a communication network

The first thing I did was set up a *communication network* with other people. The more isolated we stayed, the worse things would get. Before living alone and before my divorce, I had a network of online friends who were very supportive and helpful to me in the months leading up to this new chapter in my life. They were there 24/7, answering emails and suggesting links, organizations and outreach groups. They may have been people I could not see and have never met, but after years of knowing them online, they were my *support system* to help me through some very hard times. Their help meant the world to me, and I knew I couldn't have gotten through everything that I did without them. And just as I understood this valuable connection, I also knew I had to keep some kind of *social* connection there, now that we were by ourselves.

Because of this, I started calling up friends and family out of state as soon as my phone was turned on. Sure, this meant racking up my phone bill, but my need to reach out to people I already knew, people who I *needed* to communicate with, far surpassed my worries over the phone costs. Pretty soon, after I had Internet access, I became acquainted with a divorced mother who lived nearby via MySpace, and I started calling her, too. She'd been divorced for some time and I guess she understood my anxieties over being a newbie, because she was always there to talk with on the phone, to answer personal questions and answer messages I sent to her. She was really helpful and her friendship sure helped out a lot! Even though we lived in the same city, we unfortunately never met in person. Still, it was nice to have that shoulder to lean on while the friendship lasted. I still wish we hadn't lost touch and that we could have met in person, or that our kids could have met, but I know people come in and walk out of our lives for a reason. People are in our lives at the time they are meant to be in our lives, and sometimes, when that purpose is no longer needed, that's when our paths must go their own way. Even though I remember her fondly, I have accepted she is not part of our lives anymore and feel grateful she *was* there when I really needed a friend.

To expand my communication network, I joined a local church. I didn't make the kind of friends I'd hope to make—friends who'd stop by for coffee or to hang out with, go shopping with or invite over for dinner—but just being around other people was a huge benefit in tearing away my feelings of isolation. Just having people I knew by name or knew through the church still helped meet my needs to socialize with others.

—Get educated

Another thing I did was educate myself. I started reading books and visiting divorce-related websites. I'd often head out to the bookstore on days my daughter was with her dad, spending hours reading books about divorce. Since self-defense was a big issue for me, I knew I had to educate myself on that subject, too. I had this book called *Street Smarts,* and even though it was an old book, I decided to give it a read, anyway. One of the things it suggested a woman living on her own should do was familiarize herself with her neighborhood: "Get to know your neighbors. Cultivating a sense of community and watching out for one another may be one of the best safety precautions." (pg. 3, *Street Smarts: A Personal Safety Guide for Women* by Louise Rafkin, Harper Paperbacks, 1995).

So I got to know my neighbors and the neighborhood we lived in. I was surprised to learn one of my neighbors was a part of a local band named Grynch. (I didn't learn this right away, of course.) Three members of the band lived in the house: Darrell, Tobby and Sean. Darrell is the one I met first. All the guys were *very* nice and I even became friends with Darrell's girlfriend, Heather. I would hang out over there a lot, often while Jennifer played with the kids, and the more we talked about the area and goings-on, the more comfortable and secure I started to feel. A bonus was that Darrell knew people in the neighborhood and would point out who was who, calming my fears over some stranger lurking in the area. Everyone was very friendly, welcoming and especially patient when it came to communication snags. Darrell and Heather often resorted to writing down what they said if I couldn't lipread them. And I guess having a deaf neighbor was a bonus for them, too, because I sure couldn't complain about the noise!

Jennifer and I often went for walks, mostly so that I could become familiar with the streets and where everything was. (This was a good idea especially to learn about all the nearby streets! It took *many* cases of me getting lost many times as I drove to appointments and such before I finally became familiar with the area.)

—Change and improve locks

As for personal safety, well, that right there didn't get resolved too easily. After I'd come home to find doors I left locked unlocked, I talked to my landlord about it then ran out to buy more locks. One of those locks was a child-safe lock, and that ended up being a good investment because, one morning, I awoke to find my front door unlocked and pushed against the child-safe lock as if someone from outside had tried to break it open. Some of my sisters thought perhaps Jennifer had tried to get the door open while I'd been asleep, but I knew full well it couldn't have been her because she wasn't *that* strong to get the door forced up against the lock the way it was. I also put chairs under doorknobs and extra locks on my windows for good measure. Here again, my virtual friends came to my rescue. I talked about this concern and many of them offered pointers and tips on keeping doors and windows locked and secure. My landlord also changed the locks on both the front and back doors. After this, I no longer discovered unlocked or pushed-in doors.

I even became paranoid that the old tenants were trying to scare us away or force themselves in to recover some hidden precious heirloom they'd left behind! (I suspected the former tenants after I'd learned they still had the keys to the house!) One of my online friends, Brandon, heard about this incident and offered information on extra security measures to take: "Make sure you hang bells from the doors. That way, when someone opens it, they make noise. And get some locks for the windows, you can get them at the hardware store, just tell the man there what you want to do. If you have a sliding window to your balcony, measure the inside part where the window slides and cut a broom handle to fit perfectly in the slot. If you do it correctly, you should not be able to open the door."

Still, all those extra locks didn't help me sleep better at night. For the first few months, I *barely* slept at all. I'd wander about the house through the night, checking and rechecking the doors and windows. I did try to sleep, but that only resulted in tossing and turning for hours on end. I left certain lights on—the dining room, hallway and sometimes even the kitchen—and I'd also occasionally just sit in a chair facing the front door, my eyes never leaving it.

Sometimes, I even purposefully stayed on the computer into the wee hours of the morning, just to help me stay awake in case anyone broke in.

In fact, there were only two occasions in which I did get any sleep: On the weekends my daughter was with her dad and during the time Darrell allowed me to keep one of his 2-Way radios in the house overnight. He first suggested this arrangement after a house behind him had been robbed. He left his on and told me to radio him in case anything should happen during the night. This arrangement did a world of good for me. I felt safer and slept better knowing I had some way to *call* for help in case anybody broke in and tried to hurt us. It made me feel so much better that I asked him if it was okay to keep this arrangement for a couple of extra days.

—Have faith

I prayed an awful lot during those first few months, too. I prayed and prayed, asking God to watch over us and keep us safe. I truly believe God did indeed watch over us, because when I finally gave in to my need to sleep at night, nothing usually happened. In fact, the two things that *did* happen resulted in no one being hurt. On one night, Jennifer had been awakened by someone pounding on our front door. She went to the living room window to look outside and whoever it was saw her and took off. (She relayed this incident to me the following morning.) On another night, *thankfully* when Jennifer was with her dad, I had the foresight to keep my bedroom door locked as I slept, and I'm sure glad I did because I awoke the next morning to find books removed from the book shelf, placed on the floor, and assorted family photos moved to different positions.

—Stick together

I just could *not* sleep, however, until I changed one thing: Jennifer had to sleep in my bed with me. There was no argument there. She *had* to be close to me! Surely, I thought, if someone ended up trying to hurt her, the struggling would wake me up. This arrangement helped me feel better, too, but it was still a long time before I finally slept through the night. In fact, I kept an aluminum baseball bat next to my bed *and* one of my hunting knives under my mattress!

I also made it a point *always* to keep Jennifer in my view, and as close to me as possible, whenever we went out. I'd hold her hand all the time and never let her leave my sight. Even when she had to use a public bathroom, I'd stand outside of her stall. At home, I had child-proof locks on the doors so she couldn't just open the front door and wander off outside while I was in another room.

Additionally, I kept an eye on our surroundings when we went out. I'd notice people coming into buildings or passing us by, I'd take a good look around us before heading out into a parking lot or getting into our car, and I'd also try to remember faces of people I knew working at different locations in case someone new appeared or if something just wasn't right.

Another thing I did was take baths/showers with Jennifer. I couldn't bear to leave her alone so I could shower, even if it was a *quick* shower, so we took baths together. However, if that wasn't possible, I'd wait until she was asleep or get up early in the morning to take a quick shower.

—Be assertive and strong from within. Listen to your gut!

Despite these precautions, I knew that I also had to make myself stronger, too. It wasn't enough that my house was secure; I had to be secure, too! I had to *toughen myself up* and be more assertive. Even in the face of some of my sisters claiming I was being paranoid about the things going on around us (especially with the unlocked doors—as if I had *imagined* the doors were unlocked!), I had to be strong and just *deal* with it! If other people didn't believe me about stuff that was going on, that wasn't going to change anything. Still, building up my assertiveness was important—and also something put to the test.

One day I was busy going about the house, cleaning, when I noticed my daughter sitting on the couch next to the living room window, talking to someone outside. This stranger, who looked like a hobo because he was dirty, dressed in rags and had the stench of alcohol on his breath, came up to our window and carried on a conversation with Jennifer. I hated it that I couldn't understand what they were talking about, but I knew this wasn't good. I kept trying to distract Jennifer *away* from this sort of thing, but she wouldn't budge. Then the guy started looking at me and asking me to let him in. Despite my past of trying to be nice to people, alarm bells sounded within me and my mind was screaming, "NO WAY!" I kept politely telling him I couldn't let him in. (I even apologized, for crying out loud! I shouldn't have had to.) Again he asked me to let him in and again I said no. This whole thing went on for some time, even with the guy examining the window to see if he could remove the screen, and when he *finally* retreated from the window, I closed them both, closed the curtains then lectured Jennifer over talking to strangers.

I ended up getting a lecture, too. Later, after I told my mom about it when talking with her on the phone, she read me the riot act over how I should have told that guy off and closed the windows right away. Maybe a little assertiveness right there would have gotten rid of that guy sooner! Looking back, I realize I should have been assertive with removing my daughter from the window, too.

—Get a regular telephone and learn how to use 911

Additionally, I often had online chats with my friend, Mark, who lived in California at the time, and after I told him about the *drunk at my window* incident, he said I should've picked up the phone to call 911. Mark *knows* I am deaf and not wearing a hearing aid, but even the deaf should be able to use 911!

Problem was, I didn't know how. I had been taught in high school that I should dial 911, wait a few moments, and then repeat my name, that

I am deaf, my address and the emergency every five seconds. But, that was in high school. Had the rules changed since then? Were 911 operators instructed with new guidelines on how to handle a call from a deaf person? I really didn't know. (I talk more about calling 911 in a later essay.)

And I didn't have a phone, either. That was a big problem right there. I used Internet relay for phone calls, which only required Internet access and not a regular telephone. For situations like what happened at the window, I knew I *had* to get a phone!

So I made the choice to go out and buy a regular telephone. At least 911 emergency centers could track a call, and if I screwed up on the standard procedure for a deaf person to call 911, at least they'd know there was an emergency at a certain location. I also made it a point to teach Jennifer how to use the phone. I explained it wasn't a toy, how to dial 911 if there was an emergency, what kind of emergencies there would be, and how to answer the phone, should it ever ring. (At one point, she got confused when the caller insisted on speaking with someone, so I told her to tell them to call Paul [our landlord] and hang up.)

—Monitor Internet activities

One more security measure had to be put in place before I could breathe easy, though: What I did on the Internet. I never really paid much attention to this, but something else came about to bring this particular issue into light. One morning, I opened my front door to find some kind of homemade craft object on my doorstep. At first, I was pleasantly surprised, thinking one of Darrell's boys had made it or Heather's daughter, but when I asked them about it, they said they hadn't. I suddenly became nervous. *Who* exactly had put this thing on my doorstep? All it said was *hi* (with cake icing) and that's it. There was no name or anything. Being a girl who once lived in Los Angeles, I suddenly became suspicious. Sure, it looked innocent enough, but I wasn't playing into *that* kind of mindset. Especially with all the other things that had been going on!

I chatted online with a friend about this and she asked me to take a picture of it and email it to her. After I did that, she looked at it and became worried, too. The whole thing just didn't look innocent. We were both grateful my daughter wasn't there at the time and she cautioned me to keep an eye out for anyone hanging around my front door. She also asked about my blog, a site which was public and often contained personal information. I told her about the kinds of things I talked about on there and she said that right there was a serious no-no. She said not to put *anything* personal on my blog. In fact, make up a story about how I just got a *big* guard dog to protect the house with, and post a photo of a vicious-looking dog along with it. I ended up not doing that because I didn't feel comfortable putting a fake post on my blog unless it was for a joke for, say, April Fool's Day, but the whole warning of not getting personal with my blog was a message that got through. She had a good point. From that moment on, I was careful with what I *did* blog about online and what other online activities I did.

—Educate children about safety

Learning how to use the phone and dial 911 weren't the only things I had to teach my daughter. One fault is that my daughter is a *very* social person, and this is a fault because she has a *very* bad habit of talking to strangers. I would constantly have to remind her of the dangers of talking to strangers. It frightened her that there were strangers out there in the world who could hurt her (well, after all, she was only four years old!), but I tried to be as gentle about it as I could.

Another thing I talked to her about was what to do when someone was at the door. I instructed her to *get Mommy* if ever anyone knocked at the door, instead of answering the door herself. I'd keep an eye on her anytime she was outside, so I also instructed her to first ask for permission before going outside. (This was especially important since we lived on a busy street.) I also told her to let me know if the phone was ringing so I could sit with her when she answered it (and be aware of what she was saying).

You could say this whole change in my life really put me to the test. It was a brand new world for me to face, a brand new experience I had to get through. I am grateful I am no longer a divorced parent (her father and I reconciled and remarried), but that doesn't mean we had to stop using these measures of personal safety and assertiveness in our lives. They are important security measures for every deaf person to use!

The lessons I had to learn in how to be a confident and capable divorced parent hadn't been easy, but they were lessons to last me a lifetime.

Lessons I Should've Learned but Didn't . . .

Looking back, I realized there were certain lessons I should've caught on to while being a divorced parent. True, I can't expect to learn *everything* there is to learn about divorce in the seven months that it lasted, but I think it would have helped if I had acted on them when they came up.

—*Everybody's* safety is important

On the nights my daughter was with her dad, I threw caution at the wind. I let my guard down. I didn't take care of myself. I just didn't *care* as much about safety and security as I should have. And I *really* should have. It's not just the child who needs to be protected when a deaf parent is living on her own; Mommies and Daddies need to take care of themselves, too! I didn't really digest this important piece of advice very well. I was lucky my carelessness didn't result in something bad happening, but you never know. Anything could happen, and the divorced deaf parent living all by herself and spending the night all alone needs to be prepared and ready for *anything*!

—Get a (better) watchdog

My dog, a Chihuahua mix, slept on my bed with me, and his movements woke me up when he barked. If someone knocked at the door while I slept, he was sure to let me know! But when it *actually* came to guarding the turf when there were strangers about, he didn't act so valiant.

In fact, he'd often hide under my bed!

As much as I loved my dog, I kept struggling with this fact that he wasn't being a very good guard dog for us. Besides, he is a Chihuahua! They don't really incite the same amount of terror in someone a German Shepherd would! I know I should've tried to get a better watchdog for added protection (after all, being deaf granted me the eligibility of having a hearing dog *without* being forced to pay a pet fee or even have the dog counted as a *pet),* but I just didn't take that action. Still, I think it's something important enough that I *should* have tried to do it.

—Practice self-defense

I couldn't afford a self-defense class, but there *are* pictorial, detailed tutorials on the Internet about self-defense. These are good to use. I could only practice what little moves from Tae Kwon Do I could remember from my teen years, but I didn't do this all the time. Maybe if I had, I'd be more confident about living alone and sure of myself if I ever needed to use them.

—Join a divorce support group

Any kind of support can be helpful for someone going through a major transition in life, but with a group of other people who have been there and done that, their support can help save time and be inspiring, if not educational! My friend at church constantly suggested I try to attend a divorce support group her mother was a part of, but I was just too nervous to do it. I was too nervous about meeting strange people and *opening myself* up to them. Still, I think it would have helped. It also would have been just one more way to expand my communication network!

—Make it a habit to check and double-check *every day!*

Sure I'd check and double-check doors and windows to make sure they were locked, but I didn't do that *all* the time. This is an important habit to implement. Always check and double-check the locks! Do this before leaving the house and before going to bed. Make it a point to do it every day. My former ex-husband reminded me of how important it was to make this a habit, but sometimes, I just forgot.

Alone but Not Helpless: Finding Resources as a Divorced Deaf Parent

For nearly my entire life, I was around family members who were always ready to help. I grew up hanging out with my sisters and brothers more than I hung out with my friends! Even in adulthood, we stayed close, and whenever one of us moved to a neighboring city, chances were good some of the clan would follow.

That changed when I was 31. That year, my husband got a job in Oregon, while we were living in the California desert. The year was 2005, and even though our marriage was on the rocks, I eventually agreed to move with him, even though I had divorce on my mind. Part of me embraced this new adventure in life, but a bigger part of me ached. I'd be living so far away from my family, in a place where I knew no one. Plus, Jennifer would not be seeing her grandparents as much as she used to. She practically saw them every day. Now, she would grow up rarely seeing them at all.

It is perhaps this ache which made the adjustment so hard. It took a very long time to get used to living so far from my family, and despite my many attempts to move back even after I was divorced, that just never happened.

The security of being around my family never forced me to take charge of my own needs for resources until then. Now, after I was alone and so far away from their help, I had to figure out how to make things work on my own.

Child support had not been a part of my divorce settlement (a mistake I came to regret—it is *so important* to make child support a part of a divorce judgment!), so it came to us in bits and pieces. I have a lifetime monthly income, but it was just enough for us to survive on each month, with very little left over for savings. After weeks spent on an apartment hunt with nothing affordable in sight, I was lucky to find a 2-bedroom home for me and Jennifer that was perfect for just the two of us, for $750 a month, but the utilities factored in as another matter. Then we had groceries to buy, of course.

Occasionally, I also needed to have money for repairs (my landlord took care of preexisting repair needs), as well as the occasional medical costs associated with having a young child to care for. I didn't have insurance, but my ex was able to keep our daughter on his insurance plan.

Sometimes, I had to go without so that my daughter didn't have to. The financial responsibilities of being in charge of *everything* came as a shock following my divorce. Before I married, I was living with people—sisters, cousins, friends, a boyfriend—so I was always sharing costs. Now that wasn't there anymore. I was responsible to pay for *everything!* It was really something of a wake-up call for me. And, it wasn't easy, either. I wasn't used to living like this, so there had to be some changes.

For one thing, I had to be smart with money. I had to use coupons, shop for the cheap stuff at grocery warehouses, and change my idea of what exactly a *meal* consisted of. I lived off of Ramen Noodles a lot. Still, there were many times my heart would ache over my daughter complaining about being hungry when all we had to eat was a box of crackers.

So I made it my mission to bring in some extra income. Find some way for us to bring in more money so we wouldn't starve. Up until then, I was *always* of a mind to be a stay-at-home mom. I mean, I figured I had an annuity, and even though it's not a *huge* monthly payout, I had that so I didn't have to work. Now I was the sole breadwinner. I was the sole provider. With more financial obligations piling up around me, I knew I had to shed this way of thinking and become a working mom. I *had* to work. I had to. I was just so frustrated of *both* of us being hungry and not being able to enjoy any fun activities in life.

So I tried to get a job. My daughter and I would walk to different locations (fast food restaurants, department stores, grocery stores) and I'd fill out applications. At first, I didn't have a car, so the walking became our prime form of getting around. I'd fill out these applications even though I couldn't receive phone calls. (My TTY was broken.) My neighbor Jimmy said I could use his phone number, but nobody ever called him after I filled applications out. And believe me, I filled applications out *everywhere!* I even went to places that didn't advertise for help wanted, and I'd even call them later to check in on the hiring status. But in the end, that didn't work out very well. I guess it didn't help that I had practically zero work experience (just babysitting and odd housecleaning jobs) and that I didn't know many people to list as a reference.

The next thing I tried was looking around for any odd jobs in my area. I had to keep my search close since I didn't have a car. I talked to my friend, Heather, who lived next door, and she told me all about Vocational Rehabilitation services. She said that they would help me get a job *and* childcare *and* even provide $450 a month in food benefits. They would even pay for my job training! So I swallowed my pride (I'd been doing a lot of *that* lately!) and went there to apply for their benefits. Unfortunately, because of my annuity, they only gave me ten dollars a month in food benefits. I started spending my weekends donating plasma just so I could buy food! It wasn't a lot of money, but it did help. I also made a bigger effort to recycle. (At that time, we got a discount on our monthly trash bill if we recycled.)

My neighbor had a friend who was looking for a babysitter. The pay was meager ($12 for nine hours four times a week), but I took the job because it was better than nothing. My sisters often chided and scolded me for agreeing to work for so little money, but we were desperate and that was why I continued to work this job for 3 months. It was *because* of this job that I was able to afford Christmas presents for my daughter! (One of my sisters bought us a small artificial Christmas tree over the Internet.) And I was able to buy more food, too. That was the bigger benefit. (Growing up with six siblings, you could imagine my own parents facing tough financial times. The churches always helped us out a lot, but the local churches in Eugene weren't offering food boxes to needy families. I checked. As for Christmas, the local church provided one gift to a child in a needy family, and the Salvation Army said they couldn't help us because we weren't *needy* enough.)

I also took on another odd job: Cleaning my neighbor's house twice a week. (He was a divorced dad.) He paid me $50 a week so that, coupled with what I made from babysitting, really helped us with the food bill. He also allowed me to use his washer and dryer so I could save money going to the Laundromat every week (which cost us about $25 a week) and the work I did also went toward a piece of furniture I was buying from him. So that arrangement worked out well for us. Jennifer would watch a movie or play with her toys while I spent 16 hours a week at my neighbor's house, cleaning.

I was soon able to have a little extra money for other things we needed. It was embarrassing living in a sparsely-furnished home, so I wanted to change that. I was able to buy a couch for $50 at Goodwill and I bought a desk in *very* good condition for ten dollars, off of Craigslist. We didn't have a TV set (which I guess was a good thing since we couldn't afford cable, anyway), so my daughter and I passed our free time together reading books, doing homemade crafts and going for walks. I couldn't afford to put my daughter into a preschool, so I homeschooled her. I printed worksheets off of the Internet and created teaching opportunities using whatever was in the house or backyard.

Another thing that helped was my parents occasionally wiring us some money to help out. They couldn't do this a lot of times, and it was as much as they could send, but when they did do this, that money was a *real* big plus for us. I was able to buy more than one bag of food! Hooray! I rarely, rarely ever spent extra money on impulse purchases or *fun* things for us. Every extra cent went toward buying food. And on the rare occasions I was able to pay my rent, utilities and *still* put food on the table, with a little money left over, were times I wanted to shout with joy from the roof! These moments were rare, but they still felt good when they happened.

But it was signing up with Vocational Rehabilitation services that *really* helped. Not only did my counselor help me get ready for a job, she told me about some really great resources available to the deaf and hard-of-hearing. *Local* resources. Actual places and services I could go to. All of a sudden, my knowledge of resources for the deaf in Eugene included *interpreter services* and *disabled service centers.* She instructed me on my rights as a deaf (disabled) person and showed me what I needed to do to get the assistance I needed. She even told me about bus training. Never in my life had I ridden on a public bus. I'd always had a car or a ride. Now I was going to learn how to use public transportation! This was really helpful for a while, despite some episodes of getting on the wrong bus or being unable to figure out where I had to go when, and I was grateful for this experience of learning how to ride a public bus. Later, though, I did manage to get a car, but that knowledge of how to use public transportation is something I am still grateful for learning.

My experience with Vocational Rehabilitation was a real eye-opener for me. The more resources there were opening up to me, the more empowered and independent I felt as a deaf person. It made me realize, *Wow, I* don't *have to hide away from this hearing world. I actually have rights!* Also, being the new head of the house tore away my views of being a traditional wife and mother. It changed how I saw myself. I soon *wanted* to be this self-sufficient and independent deaf person my counselor was helping me to be.

None of that would have happened if I had kept quiet. If I had humbly accepted not being able to get a job, if I had just lived with being unable to provide enough food in the home, if I had just never asked anyone I knew if they knew of ways for me to get help or any jobs they had to offer. If I had let depression, anxiety, socializing fears and homesickness keep me locked away in my house, feeling sorry for myself, none of those extra resources would have happened. Not a single one.

I did indeed go through a period of depression and anxiety following my separation/divorce, but I had to snap out of it because my child needed me to take care of her. She was *relying* on me to provide for her, and nobody else was going to do it. It was up to *me* now to make a new life for us, one in which we got by okay, and I had to tear down all of my walls and push aside all of my pain to do what had to be done. I still missed my family and I was still afraid I wouldn't get *anywhere* in finding a job because of my deafness, but I had to try. I had to *do* something.

So I did whatever it was I could think to do. I went out there to apply for work. I talked to my neighbors and my counselor about any job leads. I read job ads and scanned the classifieds. I took any and all odd jobs I could find. Sure, it meant

I never got enough sleep and it also meant we weren't exactly making a bundle of extra money, but we did earn *some* money and that's what helped us to get by. We found a way to survive.

So many things had to change after I became a deaf divorced parent. How we lived, my expectations, how I saw myself (and women as a whole), my perceptions and even my pride. The realities of this new life hit me like a steamroller, but I never let those realities keep me down. I adopted a take-charge attitude, told myself to keep going just a little bit longer even when things were so hard and so tiring, and soon we were able to make this new life possible for the two of us.

Making Deaf Parenting Work

Any time a deaf person reveals they are a parent, they suddenly become the center of attention. The looks a deaf parent gets range from the curious, to inspiring and wary. Most of the time, the looks we get are the wary ones. We might as well be saying we're blind or completely paralyzed and doing the job of being a parent all on our own. Suddenly images of children starving to death, getting hurt and being neglected come to these people's minds and, most of the time, this is the image they have of our lives. To these people, being deaf is the same as being completely helpless. This automatically stamps a title on us: *Unfit parent.*

But it doesn't have to be this way. Deaf parenting can be hard, but it's not impossible. I know I can be a good parent, even if I can't hear. It's just a matter of finding out the best way to do it. Figure out what works best for *me.*

I have been deaf long enough to pick up on a few things. I can read body language more deeply, I am more sensitive to sound waves and vibrations and, above all else, I know the importance of being aware of my surroundings. As a deaf person, I can't rely on sound to let me know someone is behind me; I have to turn around or look around every so often to see that person standing there. Sometimes I'll feel a draft and turn to see someone standing behind me or I'll smell their perfume or cologne before I notice they are there.

This is a crucial part of being a deaf parent: I have to keep an eye on my children, because my eyes are my ears. I'm not saying I should never fall asleep, use the bathroom or take my eyes off of them for a minute. What I am saying is that I can't just let my children run around without checking on them once in a while. Checking on them *with my eyes.* Seeing that they are okay reassures me that they are okay. A hearing parent has the luxury of relying on sound to know their children are okay. I don't have that luxury.

One thing about kids is that they can get into trouble so quickly, and my children are very good at getting into trouble without even trying. On occasions such as when I'm cooking dinner, doing the dishes or writing, I set them up in the same room I am in or set them up with something that will keep them distracted (like for when I am cooking) or go into the room they are playing in every few minutes (like when I'm writing). Sometimes, if possible, I'll wait until they are sleeping. When the baby napped, I grabbed those moments to do the dishes, perform other chores, call my mother or work on my writing.

Ultimately, I'd put off the things that required my complete and undivided attention until somebody could watch the children. For example, I would wait until after my husband was home to cook a meal or do the dishes. If necessary, I'd put the baby in the high chair, just so I could keep him in view.

Also, whenever I went out with my children, I *always* kept them close by and in view. If I had to look away, I'd have a mirror set on them, or I'd place my hand on them to know they were still there.

Another thing that has helped me make deaf parenting work is the use of technology. Some of the Assisted Listening Devices (ALDs) out there are either too confusing or too expensive, but the tools I have relied on (such as the Baby Cryer) really help a lot. If anything, they make life easier.

One other thing that is very important is being able to communicate with my children. There's so much talk about teaching babies and kids how to sign but, for me, this has been one of the hardest things I've had to accomplish. But in the end, once I've got the communication problem taken care of, it'll make things *much* easier. Of course, kids can always point or use facial expressions and gestures to communicate, but I have to make it easy for my children to communicate with me. If at all possible, set up some way to communicate through sign language (or even through home signs) to keep the communication lines open.

At the same time, I have to allow my children the opportunity to enjoy the things I can't. Theirs is a hearing world. It's the world they need to truly be a part of in every way possible. My children love music. Jennifer enjoys playing her flute, guitar, keyboard and xylophone. Jesse loves to play the keyboard and dance to music. And even though I can't hear the music they make, I clap and dance along with them. These kinds of things are just harmless fun for now; they may not understand that I can't hear anything now, but they will later. For now, though, music blares in the house every day and seeing me participate sends to them the message that there can be a deaf world *and* a hearing world we can both be a part of without any troubles.

I know I can't set limitations in my children's lives just because I have to live with them. I have to allow my children to enjoy all things, even things I can't enjoy with them, because there's really no harm in at least pretending to enjoy them now. Maybe at some point, Jennifer will ask something like, "Why are you still dancing, Mommy? The song is over." But until that time, I would never stop them from enjoying music and having conversations on a normal telephone.

I have learned one very important ingredient for making deaf parenting work: KEEP LIFE NORMAL. So what if I can't hear? I can't let it stop me from enjoying life, meeting people and trying new things. I'm not going to let it get in the way of attending my daughter's talent show or my son's spelling bee.

I won't make it look like being deaf is a handicap or some kind of big secret nobody can know about. Sure, people have to communicate with me differently and I may have to rely on a third party to have phone conversations, but I am a HUMAN BEING. A human being who just happens to be a parent. A parent who just happens to be deaf.

I will enjoy life. I will enjoy my offspring. I will enjoy being a parent. Being a parent isn't about what I can and cannot hear; it's about what kind of bond I develop with my children and how I find ways to overcome obstacles. It's about finding happiness and fulfillment together as a family, a family that is a combination of the deaf and hearing world.

PART FIVE

Parenting Pauses, Take Two

First Night

"Go to the hospital now," the nurse said to me in our phone conversation. "Congratulations."

That last word sank in. Why was she congratulating me? I was only leaking water. The baby wasn't even due yet. My doctor kept saying the baby was going to be born any day now, but surely not yet!

Little did I know that the *leaking water* was a sign of something very big going on here, and that did not include my large belly. It meant my water was breaking! I was about to go into labor!

I texted my husband and let him know. Up until this point, he'd made arrangements with his work that he might have to leave at a moment's notice. He texted back to me, "I'm on my way," and by the time he got home, my pants were soaked. I actually stood there crying because my pants were wet! Well, that's what happens when something like the birth of a baby is about to take place.

Arrangements had also been made at my daughter's school for us to pick her up early when the big day came. Everyone at her school had seen me waddle through the building, my belly growing bigger and bigger as my second child grew within the womb. Now they knew what was going on when Jennifer had to leave school early that day: A new life was coming into the world!

Labor came on faster and faster as my husband drove us to the hospital and I sat in the car, wincing from pain at every turn. Nurses at Sacred Heart Medical Center in Eugene acted quickly, easing me into a wheelchair and running through the details with my husband as I was whisked away to a delivery room. After a while, my interpreter arrived and we all got so excited about how the baby was about to be born. That excitement didn't last; I soon let out a scream of pain after the needle for the epidural was inserted into my spine. Thankfully, the epidural eased the labor pains and, after several hours, my son, Jesse, was born into the world. It was the second most amazing moment of my life. There is nothing as incredible in the whole world as a baby being born. It is simply one of the most miraculous experiences to live through and see.

We all gathered together as I lay in the bed, exhausted and worn out, holding the baby as we all gushed over him. My husband took pictures, and Jennifer kept talking to her little brother and telling him she loved him.

The first night of a newborn baby's life should be uneventful and calm. As it had been with Jennifer, I expected the baby to sleep peacefully in the bed next to mine. Thankfully, the doctor and nurse had no objection to this. I thought my baby's first night would pass by peacefully as it had for Jennifer, but something eventually happened which obstructed that peace.

After some time, my husband and daughter went home, promising to return the next day.

For a long time, I just lay in my bed, smiling as I stared at my brand new baby and feeling so blessed he was in our lives.

But then I started to notice something wrong and that smile disappeared.

I sat up, looking closer at the baby to see why he was moving his head that way, why his face was scrunched up like that, and why his tiny body shook. Years of experience sounded off an alarm in my head.

"He's choking!" I cried, struggling to get out of bed and pushing the button for the nurse. I kept crying out, "He's choking! He's choking!" as I weakly tried to reach for him.

A nurse hurried into the room and went over to the baby. He was already lying on his side and she moved him further onto his side as she helped him get whatever he was choking on out of his mouth. She let me know she was taking the baby to the nursery for examination, then wheeled him out.

I sat back on the bed, my heart still pounding in my chest as the shock gradually subsided. What had just happened? Why was he choking? Was it going to be something that could happen again?

Eventually, I came back to my senses. I got my cell phone out of my purse and texted my husband, telling him what had happened. At home, he was awake, and he texted back, "Okay."

Finally, after stressful minutes that seemed like hours, the nurse came back into my room. She wrote down what had happened: Jesse had been choking on water. They ended up getting a huge amount of water out of his stomach and she said if they had not found out he had water in his stomach, he might have choked on it in his sleep.

This revelation left me numb. Of course I was grateful I was able to recognize that the baby was choking, but right then and there, if I hadn't been looking at him, if I had fallen asleep, I could have lost him.

The nurse explained that they wanted to keep Jesse in the nursery on his first night, just in case more water came up. Of course, I wanted my newborn baby in the room with me, but I knew just how close I'd come to a tragedy, and I also knew they were better capable of ensuring he'd be safe. I didn't want to start getting defensive over how this whole episode was screaming at me, "YOUR SON MIGHT CHOKE TO DEATH BECAUSE YOU CAN'T HEAR HIM!"

Of course, I knew that a baby choking can be hard to catch with your eyes, and that this was a huge thing to take care of *now*. I had to refresh my knowledge of how to tell, just by sight, if someone was choking. But that would come later. I also knew I had to put my child's needs first. Swallow that pride, swallow that argument, and do what was best for the child.

So, I agreed to let my baby sleep in the nursery on the first night of his life. I just pushed aside that defensive voice and told myself it was the right thing to do. *After all, after tonight, he'll have plenty of other nights to fall asleep alongside me, and even in the same room as me.* For now, I had to think about his safety.

I don't regret the decision, especially since they did end up having to get more water out of his mouth later on that night. For the most part, I do my best as a deaf parent. I do the things I can and try to do this parenting thing on my own. I don't want to make it seem like I'm helpless or incapable of being a good deaf parent with a hearing person's help. All the same, there *are* times we do need to swallow our pride and allow that helping hand. A child's needs must come first, and there are always plenty of other things where that pride of handling it all in the face of deaf parenting can take precedence. Still, the child's needs must always come first, and no matter how capable a deaf parent may be, there will be times to just step back and allow medical professionals or a hearing person to intervene.

Smelling Trouble

People use air fresheners to freshen up the air. I am beginning to think they can become a valuable tool for deaf parents.

One day, as I sat at the computer, doing research for an article, I started to detect a strong scent. I knew that scent right away: It was from the air freshener in the bathroom. A wave of anxiety rushed through me as I jumped out of my chair and ran for the bathroom.

Sure enough, there was my little baby boy, playing with the water in the sink.

When the kids were toddlers, we kept the bathroom door closed with an eye-latch lock at the top. However, one day my little boy had figured out how to conquer that hurdle. No lock can keep him! At two years old, he'd figured out that if he pulled a chair away from the kitchen table and maneuvered it to stand in front of a locked door, it magically transformed into the perfect stepladder for him to climb up, reach up to swing the hook out of that hole, and cry freedom.

The air freshener we kept in the bathroom had a pretty strong scent, and I'm grateful we were able to smell it from a distance. Right away, that scent in the air lets us know that, A: The bathroom door was opened. And B: Chances are pretty good someone who's not supposed to be in there unsupervised was in there unsupervised.

Another scent had given me the heads-up, or should I say the nose up, that baby was getting into something he shouldn't be getting into.

Let's go back to that visual of me sitting at the computer, this time happily typing away at a manuscript. How naive I was to think I had the chance to type one sentence without having to turn around and look to see what baby was up to. The price I paid for this foolishness was the scent of Windex wafting through the air. I ended up finding my baby in the kitchen, with a cabinet open and Windex sprayed on the dog's bed. (Fortunately, my dog survived this onslaught.)

We didn't have locks on the cabinet doors in the kitchen, because a baby gate was in place at the kitchen door. The idea was that this would work in keeping the baby out of the kitchen. Not so! He managed to climb *over* baby gates and get into whatever room he pretty well pleased. (I swear, some days, I'm convinced I've given birth to Popeye!)

But since putting an air freshener into the kitchen wasn't going to work as a scent alarm to let me know a room has been invaded by unauthorized personnel, given that the door to the kitchen was kept open, the better strategy was to baby-proof the heck out of that kitchen.

Yeah, riiight.

We inserted outlet covers on all the unused outlets. Baby figured out how to pull them all out. We used drawer guards on drawers baby is not allowed to get into. Hah! Such futile attempts to protect our precious computer software and dangerous pens and pencils was met with our son victoriously pulling those drawers open!

Was there yet hope for the deaf parent unable to use her ears to make sure all was well in the kingdom?

As far as the eye can see, and the nose can smell, air fresheners seemed to offer some kind of relief for this deaf parent's frazzled nerves. And what better way to put these to use as sniff indicators that a room had been invaded than to use different scents? Citrus went into the bathroom, vanilla in Mom and Dad's room, and mint for Big Sister's room.

Alas, the kitchen, living room, dining room and computer area were not zoned for air fresheners, since these were open spaces. Yet The Powers That Be used whatever safety precautions were available to keep dangerous items out of reach, as well as remembering to look away from the computer a little more often.

Slipping Out

One evening, while logged in at Twitter, I came across a news story link that got my curiosity. The headline read "Davenport Toddler Dies of Exposure While Visiting Relatives in Montana." I was curious as to how and why that happened, so I clicked on the link to read the story. That was a bad idea, or so I thought.

The news story explained how a two-year-old boy got outside in Montana's freezing winter weather on Christmas Eve, while his parents and relatives were sleeping. The child and his parents were visiting with relatives for Christmas. With temperatures reading at 15 degrees below zero, it was not a good time for the baby to be outside by himself, especially if he was very likely to be dressed only in his pajamas. Tragically, the baby froze to death in the snow outside. He was already dead as an ambulance rushed him to the hospital.

After reading that story, I broke down and cried. How horrible! How tragic! I kept repeating through my tears, "That poor baby," but at the same time, the story touched a nerve on a much deeper level.

Not just the fact that the toddler was two years old, as my own son was two years old at the time this happened. But the one threat I'd been struggling with for some time: The fact that the baby somehow managed to slip right out the door.

Granted, a lot of parents deal with this fear. What if my baby gets out the front door? A car could hit him. She might be kidnapped. He could get into something he's not supposed to. I imagine these parents have found a way to combat this threat, and one of those ways is listening for when that door is opened. As a deaf parent, however, that just isn't an option for me. And sometimes, I won't have the front door in view. The front door was the biggest threat, because, at that time, we lived on a busy street, with cars roaring past our house throughout the day. The back door, however, had a lock on it that you needed to use a little muscle to unlock. (My oldest child, age eight, can't even lock or unlock it.) So it's the front door we worried about, and something I especially worried about when I was sleeping.

My biggest worry: what if the baby woke up and got out the front door?

One way in which we tried to prevent this from happening was attaching a childproof lock at the very top of the door. That was fine until Jesse figured out how to maneuver the desk chair under it, climb all the way up the arms of the chair, and lift the lock to unlatch it.

Next, I tried turning the chair over and leaving it lying on the floor so that he couldn't use it to climb up and unlatch the lock. However, my son reminded me of how he was *He-Man* in another life by lifting that chair back upright. There was one occasion, during the day, when I had to run and grab hold of him right before he managed to run out the door, right after he'd used the chair to climb up, unlatch the lock and open it.

The next thing I tried to do was to stay up late until my husband got home from working at night and then go to bed. We got into the habit of how he'd stay up until the time I woke up, and given that he works in the late afternoon and evening, that was not a problem. But complications from this arrangement sprang up. First was the fact that I had to get up early in the morning to get our daughter off to school. By the time he got home and I could get to bed, that meant I'd only get about four hours of sleep. The exhaustion started to wear me down, even though I tried to catch a nap during the day. It just didn't work out. The second complication was that my husband and I had no time together. If he stayed up at night until I got up, that pretty much meant I'd be sleeping alone for the school year!

One other thing we tried was a grip stopper they have for doorknobs. It covers the knob and the baby can't turn it. Unfortunately, Jesse broke these off, so they were worthless.

Then we got stuck. We just put our faith in God to watch over our son while we slept and that seemed to be the solution for a while.

Then I read this story. I started to panic. And I had to ask myself: Could I *really* live with myself if the baby got outside while we were sleeping and got hurt? Or kidnapped? Or . . . worse?

There was *no way* I could do that. I had to think of something!

I even considered setting up a rollaway bed in front of the door, just so I could block his access to it at night. However, I knew that wasn't feasible. First of all, I'd be blocking my husband's way to get in (although he could climb the fence to our back yard and come in through the back door. But now I'm just grasping at straws here). And, second, it would only be teaching him that Mommy would rather sleep in front of a door instead of her bedroom, and not that there are some doors in this house that he is *not* allowed to unlock and open. That was the bigger picture here.

He had to learn that he's not supposed to climb up on a chair and unlock a door he can't otherwise open—unless, of course, the house is on fire and it's the only way out. This is a lesson we have managed to teach our older child, but the younger one doesn't understand such things. He doesn't understand that an emergency means it's okay to break certain house rules, just that he wants to break those house rules! (We don't even allow the older child just to walk right out the front door unless she asks for permission first.)

So, we were back to square one: How do we childproof the front door in a way a two-year-old won't be able to slip out through it?

With Jennifer, we didn't have to face such a challenge. We had the childproof lock at the top of our front door and she never, ever tried to climb up on anything to unlatch it herself. But now her brother did, and now we were racking our brains to figure out what to do about it.

One thing I did was hit the Internet. I came across one mom who said she locks her two-year-old in his room to teach him to stay in there. *Egads! What in the world!* I passed on *that* idea. One mom noted how her child often awakens at night, but she goes into her mommy's room to be with her, and not out the front door.

I had to reflect on this. I had often been awakened by Jesse in the very, very early hours of the morning when he came into my room after waking up. He'd usually fool around with the books and pens on my desk (thankfully, not writing in any of the books), or put on my shoes or Jennifer's roller skates. In fact, he'd often wake me just so he could look at me with pride, as if he was saying, "Look what I put on all by myself, Mommy!" He just always came into my room when he woke up as I slept, but how could I be sure he wasn't roaming around into the other rooms?

As his parent, I couldn't put my faith into the idea maybe he wouldn't slip out through the front door while I was sleeping. It's my job to ensure my children are in a safe and childproof environment. Part of that childproofing included taking measures to prevent him from slipping outside at night. So while I was reassured by that mother's comment, I knew I still had to find a solution.

Then I read about using a baby gate at the front door. Honestly, I had to chuckle, and I wanted to say to the writer of that article, "Have you met *my* child?"

Next up was a suggestion to use a wireless alarm. I sat there thinking, *Good idea, but what if you're deaf?* I didn't like the idea of relying on Jennifer to be awakened by the alarm that would sound when Jesse opened the front door.

On the other hand, I changed my tune after I found something else: A door stop alarm. Not only does it sound an alarm when pressure is applied to the door stop plate (attached to the doorknob), but it *stops* the door from opening!

Granted, I realize the alarm would be a nuisance to Jennifer being able to sleep, and I had this thought as I tried to find a similar device that didn't sound an alarm. However, I also had to consider that it might be best for it to sound an alarm, because Jennifer would wake me up and let me know Jesse was awake and up to mischief.

Still, as a burn survivor, one thing about this device troubled me: How fast could it be disabled if the house was on fire and we had to get out the door? Without even looking into this further, my husband listened to my concern over this once and immediately discarded this option. He said we would have to keep looking for something else.

Then one day, I brought this dilemma up in a chat I was having with an editor. We chatted often (and not just about writing!) and she had often provided sage advice on one thing or another. This time was no different. She suggested we get double-sided bolt locks for the doors.

I remembered thinking, *Huh? What bolt locks?*

I checked around and saw what she meant. It's a deadbolt lock that you lock with a key! No lever or switch. Just a key. What a great idea! I mentioned this to my husband and he liked that idea, too.

After he installed the deadbolt locks, a miracle happened. For the first time in a *long* time, I finally slept through the night. I never woke up *once* to check on the kids. I felt safe the baby would not be able to get out the front door while we were all sleeping. And you know what? He didn't. Problem solved!

That security was a sure thing at night. During the day, my son would figure out you needed a key to unlock the front and back doors and often try using my keys to do just that. I started to hide my keys on a hook inside the kitchen cabinet, and as long as he didn't see them there, we were in the clear. At least at night, his safety was assured.

Just a Text Away

Ah, texting. Old fashioned folks may look down on it, cursing the unfortunate plight of teens addicted to their cell phones or mourning how texting is ruining literacy among our future leaders. As for me, I cling to it. I shunned it at first, just as I do all new things. I don't jump on any bandwagons; I wait and watch first, just to see if something sticks around and has a good reason for being there.

Texting definitely has a good reason for being there—especially if you are deaf. And when I finally started texting, I was immensely grateful that, finally, we could communicate with a cell phone without needing to hear.

These days, I text a lot. It's like having a cell phone conversation just like everybody else has, without the actual talking and listening. Soon after I got a phone on which I could text, I started texting everyone: My husband, my neighbor, my sisters and friends. That texting ability definitely came in handy on the day I went into labor with my second child, then, later, after I got lost on the way to the hospital after my son fell and hit his head. My neighbor would text me to let me know he was at my door and my daughter's school nurse texted me when Jennifer was sick and I had to come pick her up. The fact that the phone vibrated when it went off made it easier for me to catch those texts.

Well, the vibrating feature is helpful when I actually have the phone in my pocket or close to me and in sight. There have been many times I'd keep my cell phone up on a shelf or in my purse, and these were times I missed an incoming text. I keep the volume on my phone turned high, so my children usually hear the phone when it goes off. This is when Jesse will get my attention to say, "Your phone is loud," or Jennifer will inform me I got a message. If the kids aren't around, however, and my phone is somewhere else, I have to remember to check it every so often to see if there are any new messages.

Voicemail used to be a problem for me, because of course I can't hear any of the messages left on my phone. At first, I elected to ignore these messages, since the person who was calling my phone obviously did not know me since they didn't know I was deaf, so it was no big deal. But then I later learned that teachers, schools and even secretaries at doctor offices had tried to reach me through voicemail, all to no avail. After some time, I was informed of an app available for smartphones that turns voicemail messages into a text message, putting what the person said into words. What a wonderful innovation! I have yet to find one that suits my needs for my phone but I have been told that this particular app has been immensely helpful. I could see how it could be helpful to a deaf person receiving voicemail messages. Also for voicemail, another thing we did was notice how our phone would show the number from the caller leaving a message. We would look this number up on Google and sometimes see it's a message coming from the doctor's office or a school. In this case, we'd use relay to call them back. But if we don't know the number, person calling or the business, we'd figure it was a wrong number and delete the message. (Here is another reason why I prefer email communication, because then at least a stranger has a chance to introduce him—or her—self.)

For a deaf person, texting is a godsend. As much as I am grateful we have this technology that makes it easier for the deaf to communicate with the hearing world, I know that, all the same, texting is not 100% perfect.

The thing that is not so great about texting is that, sometimes, messages don't get through right away. In a perfect world, all emails and text messages would be delivered right away. But sometimes I missed a text sent from my daughter's school hours ago only because it finally appeared on my phone or a text from my husband doesn't reach me until the next day. This delay worries me, because sometimes the texts are time-sensitive or from emergency situations. I hope someday that will be fixed or cell phone providers inform their customers on how to fix that problem.

Another thing that is not great about texting is that, even as we deaf customers may be able to call for help via texting, we may not be able to text 911. In the beginning, this was an unfortunate truth for deaf cell phone texters. We could not text 911 for help. We had to do what we were taught to do: get to a regular phone, dial 911, wait a few minutes to allow the line to ring then say into the receiver, nonstop, our name, that we are deaf, our location and the emergency. I, personally, was instructed to do this in high school. I was also told to repeat that same line several times until help arrived. For a nonspeaking deaf person using a TTY, we are instructed to dial 911, tap the space bar a few times to indicate we are a deaf caller, then hope and pray we are put through to a 911 dispatcher who uses a TTY. However, nowadays, I am reading more about how it will soon be possible to text 911 on our phones. I can only hope this will be a reality someday because there have, in fact, been a few emergencies where my daughter tried texting 911. However, she later learned how to use my smartphone to call 911, and she spoke for me when we had an emergency. All the same, it would be nice for me, the deaf parent, to be able to reach 911 on my cell phone, because what if something happens to one or both of my hearing children and I'm the only one to call for help? Let's hope technology catches up with the needs of a deaf caller. (At the time this book was being prepared for publication, I learned that there are certain measures being taken that will help people use texting for 911.)

Despite these setbacks, texting is still a great way for the deaf to communicate with the hearing world. I am grateful for this technology and hope it will be a permanent part of society—minus the addictive side effects that come with it.

A Second Pair of Ears?

I promised myself I would never do this. As far as I knew, this was a bad thing to do. It was a mistake, even perhaps a sign of weakness. Doing this thing would be a sign that I failed in making sure I could communicate with my hearing child without any help.

But I'd done it, anyway. And afterward, I kept asking myself if I had screwed up.

Jesse was going to be entering kindergarten soon, and that meant it was time to check out the elementary schools available for him to attend. Of course, my husband and I already planned on sending our son to the same elementary school Jennifer had attended, but we still had to go through the motions. We still had to fill out forms and take tours. So that was exactly what we did at my daughter's school one day. After the tour, Lana, the secretary set Jesse up with some crayons and paper while I discussed the form I had to fill out with her, and asked questions.

During this time, however, Jesse stopped coloring and looked up at us. He said something which, unfortunately, I did not understand the first time. (He'd often just talk to us instead of using any signs). Well, I thought he said, "I need to go to the toilet." I wasn't 100% sure if that is what he said; sometimes it takes me a few moments to get what someone is saying when I lipread them.

But ears that actually work are quicker, and in this case, there was another adult in the room who heard him.

When I looked at her was when I got what Jesse had said. And before I could ask her a question, she interpreted my look as a way of me asking, *A little help?* "Bathroom," she said.

I proceeded to ask her my question. "Can he leave that here?" I asked, indicating his picture.

She said yes, then guided us to a nearby bathroom.

As I followed behind them, I started to mentally kick myself that I allowed such a thing to happen. I wasn't angry at her, but I was angry at myself. I let someone think that sometimes I don't understand what my hearing children are saying to me when I try to lipread them and therefore I need someone who can hear to help me out.

This, I felt, was a Very Bad Thing. To me, this was against the rules of deaf parenting. I could not rely on a hearing person outside of the family to help me understand what the children said when there is no sign language, no writing and I can't lipread them. This was a bad idea because someone who does not understand how things are and may not understand my attempts to be a good parent would feel that I just can't hack it.

The reality is that I cannot *always* communicate with my hearing children. I try, I *do* try my hardest to communicate with them, but there are times when it just doesn't happen. Sometimes I don't get what they are saying or they just give up repeating themselves Sometimes, they *don't* want to repeat themselves, and I don't even think about asking them to sign it at that point, either.

Or there are times when there's some misunderstanding. For example, my children may not hear me very well because I'm not speaking loud enough or I may not pronounce words correctly, so there's this thought that I just didn't get what was being said. (Many times I have told my children, "That's what I said," after a failed attempt to repeat them or when I have told them something. Sometimes I think *I* am the one who needs the assistance of a speech therapist!).

But even as I was beating myself up over this communication mistake, I kept asking myself, why didn't Jesse sign? He *knows* how to sign *toilet,* and has done so many times at home. Was it possible that since he knew he was around a hearing person, it was okay to stop signing? He'd just spent a lot of time around this hearing person and talking with her without signing, so maybe what happened here was the same thing that happened with Jennifer after she'd spent time with hearing people: He forgot he needed to use sign language when communicating with his mommy.

On the other hand, this had been a problem with Jesse at home. He often did not sign to us. We do lipread our children in addition to using sign, but it is Jennifer who signs to us more than anything else. I think she just got tired of repeating herself. Jesse, on the other hand, was the opposite. He would hardly ever sign, so we resorted to lipreading him. Sometimes, we even had to rely on Jennifer to help us understand him if we could not lipread him. Another thing Jesse resorted to doing in such a situation was either drawing or writing down what he was saying. (Until he learned how to spell words correctly, we had the delightful time of trying to decipher the jumble of letters he used to spell out words.)

It's interesting how this was such a perfect example of the communication methods we use in our home: One child signs and the other child makes us lipread. Talk about a deaf/oral home!

Despite all of this, however, I cannot show this vulnerability to hearing people who don't understand how things are. Jennifer always acts as interpreter when we are out and about, but she is not with us every time we are somewhere else with Jesse. If I resort to relying on another hearing person to help me understand what my hearing child is saying, I could end up being judged harshly or even have people start reporting me for being a bad parent, just because I am deaf.

The bottom line is, we *cannot* allow this kind of thing to happen. Jesse and I do need to work out all of our communication hurdles, because I really don't like those hurdles being there. I accept that sometimes I miss a word or even a sentence my kids will say—sometimes I am just too tired to lipread them!—but I don't accept the times I may not understand Jesse and ask someone else to tell me what he said. That is just not acceptable.

Bad things that happen to us in life have a way of acting as a wake-up call. That experience at the school was like Life grabbing me by the collar and saying, "You need to do something about this!"

Something indeed was done.

Not too long after this incident, I had this happen again: I was having a hard time understanding what Jesse was saying to me. The problem, however, was that Jesse's question was not worded properly, so I instantly thought *He can't really be saying that.* Still, I had to allow for the possibility that he *was* saying that. He's five; he will sometimes ask questions that are not worded properly. It happens with children. So, the first thing I did was ask him to come closer to speak to me, since my eyesight is not all that great. Then I asked him to look right at me and say very clearly what he had asked. I did misunderstand him again and he did grow frustrated, but I calmed him down and explained I was *trying* to understand him. We resorted to him making up signs for what he was saying since he didn't know the signs for most of the words in his question. This was what resolved the problem, and I finally got his question: "Do I get school today?"

I smiled and answered, "Yes, you do *have* school today."

I'm confident that this is a solution we'll start using from now on. Just have Jesse come closer, make up signs for what he doesn't know the sign for, and look at me as he speaks each word as clearly as he can. I only hope that by using this method, it won't ever again require someone who can hear to relay to me what my child has said. I appreciate the help, but in situations like this, being able to communicate effectively with my children is more important and it's something that I just need to be able to do.

Flashing Lights and Stomping Feet

Boom!

That vibration felt familiar. I turned around, recognizing it as someone behind me stomping their foot on the floor. Sure enough, a tiny hand reached out to me and the fingers moved in an attempt to sign. This wasn't the work of someone who had forgotten how to sign; it was my two-year-old son, Jesse, imitating something he had seen his parents do in order to get each other's attention. I started to wonder: *Does he understand that the reason why those two things were done is because of deafness?* Who knows? But all I saw before me as I watched him was a child imitating something he had seen other people in this family do in our home.

Yes, we do stomp our feet to get a deaf family member's attention. It used to be that stomping a foot was a sign of anger or frustration. In fact, for the two occasions where I lost my voice, I often stomped my foot when I was angry or frustrated.

For every other occasion, however, stomping our foot mainly has one purpose: To let Deaf Mom or Deaf Dad know that their attention is needed. I noticed this early in my relationship with my husband, when he was my boyfriend. If I stomped my foot close to where he stood or sat, he'd turn to look at me. Wow, that was much better than throwing a pillow at him!

As a deaf person, it's not as easy as hearing our name called or hearing a horn going off if someone physically needs our attention. The way it's normally done is being tapped on the shoulder, having someone wave their hand or arm in our view, or someone touching our arm to let us know they are there. Or sometimes they won't do anything at all, like a kid in a department store who moved his pushcart into my back because I failed to move out of his way. He let me know, "I told you to move," without even realizing I couldn't hear him. We can't hear if someone is behind us calling our name or if a horn is going off behind us to move out of the way. We need physical cues that we can see or be made aware of through touch to let us know.

And it appears that sometimes, stomping our foot close to where the other is standing or sitting is another helpful physical cue that their attention is needed. Up until we both started using it, we'd go up to the other to tap the shoulder, touch the arm or even throw something in the other's direction. One time, as I sat watching television, a towel landing on my arm let me know my attention was needed. Another time, it was a ball of paper landing next to my hand as I sat typing at the computer.

Another way someone can get our attention? Turning a light on and off. I remember watching the movie, *Love Is Never Silent*, and noticing how the daughter, Margaret, flashed a light on and off to get her deaf parents' attention. I saw that, smiled, then said, "Yep, that's us, too!"

Sometimes, the flashing light isn't in the same room. Usually, if the curtains are open and there's too much daylight flooding into the room, flashing a light in that room to get our attention wouldn't work very well, because it would be hard to notice. It might work if that light was a lamp on a desk we're sitting at or on a table next to where we sit, but not for every other situation. However, if I noticed the light going on and off in a mirror or in the reflection of a window, I wouldn't run out of my house screaming because I thought it was haunted—I'd know it was somebody trying to get my attention. (At the same time, however, my dad scared me, completely by accident, when he flashed a flashlight through the curtain of my living room window. I hadn't known he had been knocking at the front door, so instead of thinking, *oh, Dad's here. I should let him in,* I ran off to get the boyfriend because I thought we had intruders.)

Eventually, my toddler noticed these things, too. Not just stomping his foot when he needed Mom or Dad, but flashing the light, too. We usually do this if we don't have any other way to get to the others' attention. For example, if my hands are full and I need my husband's help or attention right away, I'll stomp my foot. Or flash a light if I can't get to him. In some way, Jesse noticed how we did these things on occasion as well. He would also hit my arm if he needed me, or tug on my shirt. Now he knew that there were other ways to get his Mom and Dad's attention, too.

Flashing the light is just one of those ways. The other is the *boom*! *boom*! *boom*! of a stomping foot. Whatever works is whatever he'll use, just as his big sister uses them, too.

It's all part of the way life rolls in our deaf and hearing home.

APPENDIX A:
Deaf Homeschooling Mom

The following are some of the blog posts I made which detailed just how I, a mom with no training as a teacher and completely clueless on how to be a competent teacher to my preschooler, if not a deaf one, figured out little ways to homeschool my child.

Later, both of my children were in preschool, so I normally blogged on non-school days or during our vacations when I set up reading schedules or craft projects for them.

Monday, September 11, 2006

I never thought I'd take on homeschooling. I'd decided long ago that I wouldn't do it. I worried too much about my daughter's social skills, despite many homeschooling parents sharing how they met that challenge. I figured I could do it, too, but I didn't think I could do it enough.

But, because of my finances, I had to take on homeschooling my daughter. She won't be 5 until next month, so she can't enter (free) kindergarten. I can't afford the preschools, so I'm homeschooling her.

The first thing I had to do was get past my anxiety over being able to do this. I don't have a college degree. I don't have any special training.

But since my daughter's preschooling was either this or nothing, I'd HAVE to do it. Fear or no fear.

The next thing I had to do was educate myself on how to go about doing this. I scoured the Internet, checking Web sites and downloading worksheets specifically for preschoolers. I came up with a *curriculum* and decided not to spend more than 4 hours a day homeschooling my child.

Bonus: It could be ANY PART of the day. My daughter and I are not morning people (we're both night owls LOL), so we could start school at 10 a.m., if we wanted to.

Today, though, on her first day, we started at 5 p.m. I worried about this, but that worry disappeared after only 30 minutes of schooling passed.

Wait a minute. Just THIRTY MINUTES??

Yup.

And we did all the subjects, too. English, reading, math, art and *chorus*. (I'm going to include science on Tuesdays and Thursdays.) She'd already had P.E. with me earlier when we played ball, AND she played with her friend for several hours, as well. So I thought that was enough.

I didn't stretch out each subject. With English, for example, we're working on one letter a week, and today's lesson had her tracing a capital *A* and lowercase *A*. (When I asked her to write a little *A* on a sheet of paper, she smiled then wrote a tiny capital *A*. The goof.) She had trouble drawing the little *A* by herself, without the worksheets, but with gentle coaxing and practicing, even asking, "Do you want to see how I draw the little *A*?" then showing her exactly how to draw it, she finally managed to draw it herself. Throughout the lesson, I had to mentally repeat a mantra from one homeschooling article I'd read online: "Be patient!"

When I felt she had completed that lesson to satisfaction, learning and practicing, we moved on to art, then math. During the math lesson, I asked her to verbally count to ten. Now, I may be deaf, but I happened to notice when she missed *six* during her counting. From there, we had chorus and story time. We talked about how *Twinkle, Twinkle, Little Star* was different in the song and book, and when I asked her how she would make the story different, she said she would put in a princess and an orange fire-breathing dragon. (I wondered how the star fit in with all of this.) We talked about how other songs were different from the way they were told in storybooks, and I asked her which she liked better.

The thing is, she doesn't call me *Mom* when I'm schooling her. She calls me *teacher.* That definitely makes me smile. In a way, all parents are teachers to their children, but actually being called *teacher* when acting in this capacity really touched me in a way I hadn't expected. It made me feel that maybe I'd be able to find it within me to do this job pretty well after all.

Tuesday, September 12, 2006

Since Jennifer has her science lessons on Tuesdays and Thursdays, I'd have to figure out just how I'd teach someone so young a science lesson.

A search on the 'Net helped me understand it doesn't have to be anything all that difficult.

In fact, teaching preschool science could be done easily from home. I explored many sites and lesson plans until I finally decided on one that explored shadows.

And once we got started, I caught on to how easily it could be done, and how it could be a learning experience all wrapped in to one. (Now, see, it's that *natural* teacher kicking in.)

We went outside and I was grateful it was a sunny day. We stood in the backyard examining our shadows. I asked Jennifer, "What makes a shadow?"

She smiled and, pointing up, she said, "The sun!"

"That's right. When the sun is shining on you, it will make a shadow appear. Do you know what else can make a shadow?"

She shook her head.

"Light," I answered. "When light is shining on you like the sun, you'll see your shadow on the floor or the wall."

I then asked her to notice where her shadow was (in front of her) and I asked her, "How come your shadow is right here and not over there?" I pointed to her side.

She thought a minute, looked in the sky, then said, "Because the sun is right there."

Wow. Smart kid. "Very good," I replied. "If the sun is in back of you, your shadow will be in front of you. If the sun is in front of you, your shadow will be behind you." I then demonstrated, asking her to turn around. She did and I told her to look behind her to see her shadow. (Had to make sure she didn't turn around completely to do it.)

I also asked her to touch her shadow and I asked, "Did your shadow do anything different when you moved?"

"It moved, too," she said.

"That's right," I said. "If you move, your shadow moves." Then I demonstrated again, asking her to watch her shadow while she moved her arms up and down, wiggled them in the air and walked side-to-side.

Next I asked her to jump over my shadow and asked why her shadow moved and mine didn't. I told her it's because I stood still while she moved, so my shadow stood still, too.

Then I had her stand under an umbrella at the patio table and I asked, "Can you see your shadow now?"

She looked down, then shook her head.

"That's because the umbrella's shadow is covering it up," I said. I pointed at both the sun and umbrella. "The sun shines on the umbrella to make the umbrella's shadow. But when you stand under the umbrella, it's bigger than you are, so you can't see your shadow."

Next I asked her to stand under a tree. "Do you see your shadow?" I asked.

She looked down and shook her head.

"Do you know why?"

She pointed. "Because the sun can't get through."

"Very good," I smiled. "Buut . . ." And I held my hand against the house, where it was still under the tree but my shadow was visible. "Look. Can you see the shadow of my hand?"

She smiled, nodding.

"And why can you see it?"

"Because the sun got through the leaves," she answered, pointing.

"Excellent. The sun is peeking through those leaves, so you can make a shadow right here. You try."

Then she put her hand in the same spot, making her shadow appear. I asked her to move it to the left a little, where there was no sun. "How come you can't see your shadow now?" I asked.

She shook her head, looking at me. "There's no sun."

"Very good."

Next I put water into two glasses, one clear and one dark. I set them out separately in the sun. First the transparent one. "Can you see the water in the shadow?" I asked.

Smiling, she nodded.

"And why can you see it?"

"Because it's light," she answered.

"That's right. Now watch this." I put the dark cup of water down. As predicted, we couldn't notice any liquid inside. "Can you see the water's shadow with this one?" I asked.

She shook her head.

"And why not?"

"Because it's dark."

I started feeling giddy inside. "Very good, Jennifer. You're a smart scientist!"

The next thing we did was talk about how some shadows look like something when they are really something else. I held my hand up against the house. "What's that a shadow of?" I asked.

"Your hand," she replied, pointing.

Then I folded my hands in such a way. "That looks like a rooster, doesn't it?" I asked.

Smiling, she nodded.

"But it's not really a rooster, is it?"

She shook her head and pointed. "It's your hands."

"That's right. It's my hands." Next I held up a book. "What does this look like to you?"

"A book."

"Can you tell it's a book in the shadow?"

She studied both, then shook her head.

"What does the shadow look like?"

"A square."

"That's right. It looks like a square. You can't see the pages like you can on the book, right?"

We did the same thing with a candle.

Finally, I talked to her about how shadows are like an *outline* of things. Like somebody drew around something and colored it all black.

"Can you see your hair in your shadow?" I asked.

Looking down at her shadow, she nodded.

"Can you see what color is your hair?"

Maybe if she had black hair, she'd guess it right. But her hair is brown, so she didn't see that.

Next I asked her if she saw her shorts in her shadow. She nodded.

"Can you see what color your shorts are in your shadow?"

She looked down at her yellow shorts then at the shorts she saw in her shadow, then shook her head.

"Shadows don't have color. They're just an outline of everything."

Today's lessons lasted longer—and they were a lot of fun, too. In fact, she liked the water trick so much, she wanted to see it again and again. I'm glad I was able to make her science lesson fun—for both of us.

Wednesday, September 13, 2006

Even if I wasn't homeschooling my daughter, I've realized there are moments in everyday life that can be teaching opportunities. Normally, I pick up on this if she's watching one of her educational TV shows, but I have also noticed other teaching moments, as well—outside of her normal schooling hours.

This morning we had pancakes for breakfast. She helped me to make them. I asked her, "We need 2 cups of mix; can you find 2 cups on this measuring cup?" And I also let her pour, stir and flip. She had trouble with the flipping at first, but then she got the hang of it.

Next, during story time I was reading her the Disney version of The Prince and the Pauper, I paused at the part where Pluto knew that Mickey wasn't really Mickey because of his scent.

"Does Pluto look happy in the picture?" I asked.

She shook her head.

"Does Goofy look happy?" I asked next, pointing.

She nodded.

"Why do you think that Pluto isn't happy?"

She thought for a minute, than shrugged.

"Because he knows that's not Mickey," I answered, then I read that part of the story again.

"See, baby? Pluto could smell him, and he knew that wasn't Mickey because he didn't smell like Mickey."

"Oh," she said, smiling.

Then I talked with her about how dogs have a very strong sense of smell and that everybody has their own kind of smell. After a dog gets used to someone's smell, he won't bark at them anymore.

"That's why Chewie doesn't bark at your friend anymore, when she comes over," I concluded. "He's used to her smell."

So we continued the story and the rest of her lessons for the day.

I kept an eye out for other little moments to teach her something new. Whether or not it's for schooling, it's always a good parenting habit to enforce.

Thursday, September 14, 2006

This is *A* Week, and I've got plenty of *A* words to associate with this week. Anxiety. Assurance. Accomplishment. Anticipation. Advocacy.

And adaptable.

I never realized just how UNprepared I was for this homeschooling business. I learned today just HOW important it is to figure out ways to meet my daughter's educational needs. I thought it was enough to figure out what subjects to teach and for how long, and that her lessons would be every day of the week (contrary to normal preschool hours, which are actually less continuous for some pupils). But, alas, it would happen that I just don't have enough supplies needed for her math, English, science and art lessons. I have made use of the Internet—downloading worksheets and picking up on lessons here and there to incorporate—but I just don't have the supplies and extra materials for her homeschooling needs.

To improvise, I've had to get creative. For her socializing needs, for example, I take her to PlayLand, where she plays with other children for at least an hour almost every day of the week. That is also where she can do arts and crafts, so if I don't have anything for an art project for her to do (like I did today), then PlayLand meets this need, as well. I also had to create the flashcards for her math lesson today, as well as use the English worksheets I made which she has been working on all week. Additionally, I bought cheap 99-cent stickers for her beach art projects, as well as changing supplies for projects if I can't find/afford something.

I've also restructured lessons on the 'Net, changing them to accommodate my daughter's educational level. For example, if a preschool science lesson involves naming the parts of a plant, I'll break that down for her in a way that she can not only easily grasp the words, but also remember them by writing them down or drawing them.

Where I can't do a lesson with her because I don't have the materials or know how to get somewhere or can't afford a trip to an aquarium (we've been studying the beach and marine life themes all week), then I'll print stuff off of Web sites and throw it together as an improvised project. The same theme is still being taught, but until I get organized better and get more materials, I can't teach them the same way everybody else does.

Friday, September 15, 2006

Today was *grab bag day,* meaning we didn't follow a structured lesson plan like always. We DID explore learning English, math, science and reading, but it was done through *out of the norm* tasks.

Since this was *A* week, I was going to take Jennifer to the aquarium. But the last window of time we had to get there (it's a 2 1/2 hour drive), I looked out my window and saw a storm going on outside. I thought, *I'm not driving in that weather!* So, later, after the rains stopped, we went to a pet store instead to see some animals.

We had fun at the pet store. We saw rats, mice, some fish, birds, dogs, cats, snakes, lizards, guinea pigs and turtles. Jen liked checking out the turtles, and the snake that kept slithering up its tank kept scaring her.

We also saw an interesting animal today; a Russian legless lizard. I had never known there WAS such a thing as a legless lizard! We both thought it was really neat.

We also talked about animals that start with the letter *A,* and Jennifer also did this big beach art project. I had printed and cut out pictures of things on a beach—seashells, a crab, starfish, sand dollars, a sand castle and a seagull—and glued them to cardboard paper. (Jen liked looking at pictures of starfish online. There were some BIG ones!!) Then we drew a BIG picture of the beach and she arranged how she wanted everything to appear. Those got taped down, then colored. She's really proud of it and wanted it up on the wall. I have to get tacks for that; tape won't hold that big picture UP! LOL

But, it was a fun day. And that's what the *grab bag days* are all about: Having fun with learning.

Friday, September 22, 2006

This is a *recap* post. I was unable to get online for Monday evening and all day Tuesday, which is why I couldn't update this blog this week.

On Monday: My back went out on me. :(I was in too much pain to do my daughter's lessons. The pain did not subside until late that evening.

Tuesday's lessons went well. For science, we talked about how animals were different and I used flash cards and picture books to illustrate hooves/claws/paws/feet, tails, living environments and types of food. Later that day, she told her dad how she learned that some animals, like the dog, are tame, and some, like a lion, are wild. For reading, I read her the book *The Cat in the Hat.* When she was a baby, it was her favorite book. She asked me to read it so many times. It's still her favorite; I read it to her twice that day.

Wednesday: My daughter normally gets a week-long English packet to do a little work in each day. She completed the whole thing that day, however, I really think I scheduled the lessons at the wrong time of day (late afternoon) and she ended up pushing herself on that packet because she became really grouchy and irritable. She turned into a very unpleasant student, tearing up papers, writing on the table and ignoring her teacher (me). She got her first letter home and she burst into tears when her dad asked her why she did this and why she did that. I felt horrible. :(But I realized I can't let her push herself even if she thinks she can do it because she'll end up feeling overwhelmed. I also think timing is EVERYTHING with these lessons. Earlier in the day might be a better time to do them; she won't be so tired and harried from the long day's activities.

I picked up on this the next day. She was very moody and cranky on Thursday, so we skipped her lessons again this week. I think the breaks are good for her.

Today is *grab bag day*. We are going to go to the store to work on her math skills. No adding and subtracting at this point; just number recognition.

Thursday, September 28, 2006

Today I used the flashcards with Jennifer's math assignment. We're still doing number recognition of numbers 10-20. That didn't go over very well last week, so it's getting done again this week. At first she did fine counting off each number, but when I selected random numbers, like I normally do with this lesson, she got a little confused. I tried showing her a little trick, like using the number in a *teen* number to help her identify which one it is (like *thra* with *three* and *thirteen* and *four* in *fourteen* and how the one in front of a number makes it a *teen number*), but she didn't catch on to that very well. (In hindsight, I realize

I should have said *thir* instead of *thra.* No wonder the poor kid couldn't figure it out.)

I got a little frustrated, but reminded myself to STAY PATIENT! I kept my voice calm and avoided saying *no* when she guessed. Instead, I said, "Well, do you think that's correct?" or "Let's look at this number again." I get a feeling saying no has a negative affect when talking with people (that's just me and my penchant for constructive word choice in my communicating with others seeping in there!), and I tried to spend time on each number so she could think about it.

I didn't let that lesson drag on for too long. She got visibly frustrated. So I said we would work on the flashcards more later and that she did very well on today's math lesson.

She did, however, do excellent work on her English lesson. She got an *A* on all of her worksheets. I was impressed. She DOES have a tendency to write out all uppercase letters instead of lowercase, but at least she's getting her words right and no trouble with writing the letters. Apparently, she's taken after me: Strong in English, poor in Math. *sigh*

All the same, I'm keeping another reminder at hand: She's learning at her own pace. And I really have no problem with that at all—especially when guilt tries to get the better of me.

Monday, October 02, 2006

This week, we're working on basic, non-school lessons. The areas we're focusing on are Jennifer learning how to tell time, learning how to tie her shoes, learning about the different seasons and some basic problem-solving with organizing tasks. We're also still going to work on the English lessons, as well.

Today, we used flashcards and worksheets for telling time. Jennifer caught on to the hour times pretty well, but it will take time to cover the other areas. She also did some connect-the-dot worksheets and color assignment papers (like color by number).

APPENDIX B:
Resources for Deaf Parents

Organizations:

Disability, Pregnancy and Parenthood International
336 Brixton Road
London, UK
SW9 7AA
Phone: 020 7263 3088
http://www.dppi.org.uk/index.html

Deaf Parenting UK
c/o Gary Morgan
49 Gordon Square,
London
WC1H 0PD
SMS: 07928 842 529 (NEW from 7th March 2011)
Fax: 0871 2643323
Email: info@deafparent.org.uk
http://www.deafparent.org.uk/

Hands & Voices
PO Box 3093
Boulder CO 80307
(303) 492-6283
Toll Free: (866) 422-0422
http://www.handsandvoices.org/

National Association of the Deaf
8630 Fenton Street, Suite 820
Silver Spring, Maryland 20910
http://www.nad.org/
TTY: 301.587.1789
Voice/VP: 301.587.1788 or 301.328.1443
Fax: 301.587.1791

Center on Deafness
3444 Dundee Rd.
Northbrook, Illinois 60062
Voice: (847)559-0110
FAX (847)559-8199
TTY: (847)559-9493
http://www.centerondeafness.org/

Hearing Loss Association of America
7910 Woodmont Ave, Suite 1200
Bethesda, MD 20814
Phone: 301.657.2248 Fax: 301.913.9413
http://www.hearingloss.org/

Orange County Deaf Advocacy Center
1001 N French Street #8
Santa Ana, CA 92701
(714) 699-3323 Voice
(949) 955-0054 Fax
ocdac@deafadvocacy.org
http://www.deafadvocacy.org/

Deaf & Hard of Hearing Services
4328 Kalamazoo St SE
Grand Rapids, MI 49508
V: 616-732-7358
VP: 616-828-0186
Fax: 616-732-7365
http://deafhhs.org/
email: info@deafhhs.org

DEAFWORKS
P.O. Box 1265
Provo, UT 84603-1265
USA VOICE RELAY: (800) 855-2881
UTAH VOICE RELAY: (888) 735-5906
TTY: (801) 465-1957
FAX: (801) 465-1958
Internet: www.deafworks.com
email: info@deafworks.com
http://www.deafworks.com/

Scottish Council on Deafness
Central Chambers Suite 62
(1st Floor)
93 Hope Street
Glasgow G2 6LD
Tel: 0141 248 2474
Text: 0141 248 2477 & 1854
SMS: 07925 417 338
Fax: 0141 248 2479
Email: admin@scod.org.uk
http://www.scod.org.uk/

Websites:

DeafRead: http://www.deafread.com/
AllDeaf.com: http://www.alldeaf.com/
DeafNotes.com: http://www.deafnotes.com/
DeafSpot: http://www.deafspot.net/
Deafweekly: http://www.deafweekly.com/
Global Deaf Connection: http://www.deafconnection.org/
DeafNation: http://deafnation.com/
Deaf Newspaper, LLC: http://www.deafnewspaper.com/

Books:

Hands of My Father: A Hearing Boy, His Deaf Parents, and the Language of Love by Myron Uhlberg
On the Fence: The Hidden World of the Hard of Hearing by Mark Drolsbaugh
Confessions of a Lipreading Mom by Shanna Groves
A Loss for Words: The Story of Deafness in a Family by Lou Ann Walker
Train Go Sorry: Inside a Deaf World by Leah Hager Cohen
Deaf Child Crossing by Marlee Matlin
Mother Father Deaf: Living between Sound and Silence by Paul Preston
In This Sign by Joanne Greenberg
On the Edge of Deaf Culture: Hearing Children/ Deaf Parents by Thomas H. Bull
Signing in Puerto Rican: A Hearing Son and His Deaf Family by Andres Torres

The Child Care Book Especially for Parents who are Deaf and Hard of Hearing; Book 1: Baby is Here! by Mary Kay Stranik, Mary F. Nelson, Virginia Meyer, and Karen R. Lief
A Journey into the Deaf-World by Harlan Lane, Ben Bahan, Robert Hoffmeister
A Place of Their Own: Creating the Deaf Community in America by John Vickrey Van Cleve, Barry A. Crouch
Deaf in America: Voices from a Culture by Carol Padden, Tom Humphries
What's That Pig Outdoors?: A Memoir of Deafness by Henry Kisor, Walker Percy (Foreword)
The Story of My Life by Helen Keller
Deaf Culture Our Way: Anecdotes from the Deaf Community by Roy K. Holcomb, Thomas K. Holcomb, Samuel K. Holcomb
Crying Hands: Eugenics and Deaf People in Nazi Germany by Horst Biesold, Henry Friedlander (Introduction)

Movies:

Love is Never Silent
Beyond Silence
Sound and Fury
Bridge to Silence

Bibliography

"Deaf designer baby—the issues," BBC News, April 8, 2002, http://news.bbc.co.uk/2/hi/health/1916812.stm

"A Baby, Please. Blond, Freckles—Hold the Colic," by GAUTAM NAIK, *The Wall Street Journal,* FEBRUARY 12, 2009

"Deaf demand right to designer deaf children," by Sarah-Kate Templeton, *The Times,* September 23, 2007

"'Designer' babies with made-to-order defects?" Associated Press article, December 21, 2006, http://www.msnbc.msn.com/id/16299656/
Blog post "IVF Deaf Babies Not Welcome in America" on the blog of Mishka Zena, November 26th, 2007, http://www.mishkazena.com/2007/11/26/ivf-deaf-babies-not-welcome-in-america/

"Lesbian couple have deaf baby by choice," *The Guardian,* April 8, 2002
Absolute Write Water Cooler, thread "Is there a name for this?"
located at http://absolutewrite.com/forums/showthread.php?t=97351

About the Author

Dawn Colclasure is a writer who lives in Oregon. Her articles, essays, poems and short stories have appeared in several newspapers, anthologies, magazines and E-zines. She is the author of fourteen books, among them *BURNING THE MIDNIGHT OIL: How We Survive as Writing Parents; 365 TIPS FOR WRITERS: Inspiration, Writing Prompts and Beat The Block Tips to Turbo Charge Your Creativity; Love is Like a Rainbow: Poems of Love and Devotion* and the children's book *The Yellow Rose*. She is co-author of the book *Totally Scared: The Complete Book on Haunted Houses.*

WEBSITE: http://dmcwriter.tripod.com/
BLOG: http://dawncolclasureblog.blogspot.com/
TWITTER: https://twitter.com/dawncolclasure
FACEBOOK:
http://www.facebook.com/dawn.colclasurewilson
MYSPACE:
http://www.myspace.com/dawncolclasure
OTHER: http://greenwolf103.deviantart.com/

Lightning Source UK Ltd.
Milton Keynes UK
UKOW04f0738180717
305532UK00001B/85/P

9 781619 501942